Responsible Classroom Management for Teachers and Students

J. ALLEN QUEEN

University of North Carolina at Charlotte

BETH B. BLACKWELDER

Charlotte-Mecklenburg Schools

LEON P. MALLEN

University of Vermont

Merrill,
an imprint of Prentice Hall
Upper Saddle River, New Jersey   Columbus, Ohio

Library of Congress Cataloging-in-Publication Data

Queen, J. Allen
    Responsible classroom management for teachers and students / J. Allen Queen,
Beth B. Blackwelder, Leon P. Mallen.
       p. cm.
    Includes bibliographical references and index.
    ISBN 0-13-442336-4
    1. Classroom management—United States. 2. Child development—United States.
3. Behavior modification—United States. 4. Responsibility—Study and teaching. 5.
Schools—United States—Sociological aspects.   I. Blackwelder, Beth B. II. Mallen, Leon
P. III. Title
    LB3013.Q44   1997
     371.18024—dc20   96-16190
                                                  CIP

Cover photo: R. Wickham
Editor: Debra A. Stollenwerk
Production Editor: Julie Anderson Peters
Photo Researcher: Dawn Garrott
Design Coordinator: Jill E. Bonar
Text and Cover Designer: Susan Frankenberry
Production Manager: Pamela D. Bennett
Director of Marketing: Kevin Flanagan
Advertising/Marketing Coordinator: Julie Shough
Electronic Text Management: Marilyn Wilson Phelps, Matthew Williams, Karen L.
   Bretz, Tracey Ward

This book was set in Kuenstler by Prentice Hall and was printed and bound by R.R.
Donnelley & Sons Company. The cover was printed by Phoenix Color Corp.

© 1997 by Prentice-Hall, Inc.
Simon & Schuster/A Viacom Company
Upper Saddle River, New Jersey 07458

Photo credits: Scott Cunningham/Merrill/Prentice Hall, pp. 12, 47, 68, 73, 85, 129;
Barbara Schwartz/Merrill/Prentice Hall, pp. 56, 109; Anne Vega/Merrill/Prentice
Hall, pp. 1, 38, 83, 105, 114, 117, 147, 151, 163; Tom Watson/Merrill/Prentice
Hall, pp. 7, 64, 145; Todd Yarrington/Merrill/Prentice Hall, p. 106.

Printed in the United States of America

10 9 8 7 6 5 4 3 2 1

ISBN: 0-13-442336-4

Prentice-Hall International (UK) Limited, *London*
Prentice-Hall of Australia Pty. Limited, *Sydney*
Prentice-Hall of Canada, Inc., *Toronto*
Prentice-Hall Hispanoamericana, S. A., *Mexico*
Prentice-Hall of India Private Limited, *New Delhi*
Prentice-Hall of Japan, Inc., *Tokyo*
Simon & Schuster Asia Pte. Ltd., *Singapore*
Editora Prentice-Hall do Brasil, Ltda., *Rio de Janeiro*

Preface

The Responsible Classroom Management (RCM) plan is based on our educational viewpoint that all children can succeed in school. The conviction that all children can be taught responsibility is a tenet that is deeply rooted in our professional belief systems. Reinforcing these beliefs, the RCM plan requires responsible teachers and staff to deliver quality instruction in an interactive learning environment that is safe, orderly, and inviting.

The RCM plan has been successfully field-tested in numerous classrooms and schools at the elementary, middle, and secondary school levels throughout the United States. Administrators and teachers are ready to use a plan that expects students to be responsible for their success and behavior. They want to teach children to accept responsibility for their actions.

The RCM plan is a classroom, team, or schoolwide program that, when used appropriately, returns the control of classroom management to the teacher while assigning accountability for learning readiness and self-discipline to students. We believe that attempting to change or control inappropriate behavior by external means is less effective than using internal techniques that allow students to experience the logical consequences of their actions and to change their behavior themselves. The RCM plan expects strong academic performance and appropriate behavior.

The RCM plan is based on the following principles:

- For students to be responsible, teachers must be responsible.
- Responsibility is taught and incorporated instructionally throughout the year.
- The classroom environment is warm and inviting.
- Instruction is interactive, and student classroom participation is high.
- Standards and guidelines replace rigid school and classroom rules.
- Children are treated fairly but not always disciplined in the same manner.
- Consequences are used to teach students to self-correct inappropriate behaviors and to assume responsibility for their actions.
- Student performance and responsibility are encouraged and acknowledged. Bribery and predetermined rewards are not used.
- Students practice internal behavior control.

iii

THEORETICAL FRAMEWORK

The book begins by providing theoretical and practical background information on the stages of child development and how relationships with significant individuals influence student behavior. A historical perspective on classroom management describes the most commonly used models and their limitations in addressing the needs of the modern student. In addition, research findings from pilot schools throughout the United States are cited. Specific techniques for replacing rules with democratic standards and guidelines and the use of logical consequences for students to self-correct behavior are explained. Two of the major elements of the program are the Intensive Care Unit (ICU) and Behavior Improvement Agreements (BIAs). These two techniques are used to remove disruptive students from the classroom environment for short periods of time until those students begin the process of self-correction. Sample forms used in conjunction with these techniques are provided in Chapter 5 and the Appendixes.

ORGANIZATION OF THIS TEXT

The book is divided into five chapters. In Chapter 1, we establish an understanding of the roots of RCM. The chapter presents the context in which RCM's theories and practices operate. During the twentieth century, numerous theories of classroom management have been formulated. As a result, teachers and administrators have had the opportunity to test the viability of a wide variety of ideas in the classroom. In this chapter, we review several models of those classroom management schemes that have been widely used. We discuss the relationship of RCM to the previously developed practices. Additionally, we examine Thomas Gordon's supportive model, Teacher Effectiveness Training; Rudolf Dreikurs's social discipline model; William Glasser's control theory model; Saul Axelrod's behavior modification model; Jane Nelsen's positive discipline model; and the assertiveness model of Lee and Marlene Cantor. These theories and practices traverse a continuum from teacher-centered to student-centered, and we demonstrate the relative position of RCM practices on this continuum. RCM's hierarchical approach to problem solving is defined within this context. Social environment and the effects of poverty on children are also presented.

In Chapter 2, we continue to establish the roots and context of the RCM approach to classroom management. This chapter emphasizes the theories of human development that are the basis of RCM's formulation—the work of Freud, Erikson, Kohlberg, and Piaget. We discuss the psychological, sociological, and physical characteristics that children bring to the classroom at important stages of their development. We explore the view that children develop according to well-established patterns but simultaneously retain a strong and persistent individuality. We show that behavioral predictability and the use of formulaic, prescribed management practices have questionable merit. Additionally, we demonstrate that the RCM plan establishes the teacher as a professional decision maker whose judgment is fundamental to successful classroom management. Finally, we present our perspective on the factors that affect behavior and the characteristics of a child with developmental impairments.

In Chapter 3, we present and expand on the principles on which RCM is based. We present and analyze our research findings from elementary, middle, and secondary schools throughout the United States. This program has been successful in urban and rural schools throughout the nation. The most significant findings follow:

- The use of RCM lowers office referrals by 80%
- RCM allows faculty to work as a team
- RCM forces students to be responsible for self-discipline
- RCM corrects hall and lunchroom behavior
- RCM basically eliminates tardiness

We discuss these findings in a practical manner. We also provide suggestions for incorporating responsibility concepts through classroom instruction.

Although many schools may be safe and orderly, few are inviting. And school violence is increasing. In Chapter 3, prospective teachers, classroom teachers, and administrators are directed in specific techniques to design an inviting environment that will reverse the trend toward increasing violence. For many students, schools are uninviting. RCM reverses this process.

Chapter 4 contains directions for using standards, guidelines, and consequences correctly. In the RCM plan, rules are not used. Instead, teachers use standards and guidelines. Standards define the general direction of the desired behavior. Guidelines provide specific guidance toward successfully meeting those standards. Standards formalize social and academic expectations. Standards can be cooperatively designed by students and faculty. Logical consequences are used rather than sequential, unrelated consequences.

In the hospital when patients require more than routine nursing care, they may be sent to intensive care for closer monitoring. We recommend the same for students who do not respond appropriately to logical consequences prescribed within the classroom, hall, or lunchroom. No longer should educators tolerate misbehavior that students elect not to correct. The goal of the Intensive Care Unit (ICU) is to help students refocus and receive guidance from the teacher or another appropriate professional staff person before returning to class. If students refuse to correct their behavior after several attempts at using intensive care, a teacher- or principal-prepared Behavior Improvement Agreement (BIA) is written in contract form as the last step before suspension or possible legal action. In Chapter 4, we

focus on the most difficult types of students in the schools today and spec-
ify the role of the Discipline Review Committee (DRC).

In Chapter 5, we describe procedures and provide models for using
the RCM plan at the elementary, middle, and secondary school levels.
Team and individual classroom models are also presented. In addition, this
chapter details a step-by-step procedure that schools or individual teachers
can use to move from their current discipline program or model to the
RCM plan.

We hope that the RCM plan will be used in any professional situation
that will help students gain the skills of responsibility. The book can be
used by professors in teacher education courses, both undergraduate and
graduate classes, and for staff development in schools and school systems
desiring to improve student discipline.

ACKNOWLEDGMENTS

We thank our reviewers for their helpful comments: Frank D. Adams,
Wayne State College; Karen J. Agne, State University of New York, Platts-
burgh; Jeri Jo Alexander, Auburn University at Montgomery; David M.
Balzer, University of Toledo; John Bertalan, Hillsborough Community College; Karen Bosch, Old Dominion University; Sandra L. DiGiaimo, University of Scranton.

We also extend our appreciation to all of the RCM National Pilot
Schools that provided direction in assisting us in the field testing of the
plan. Special recognition is given to the administration, faculty, and staff of
the following schools for permitting on-site instruction and assessment of
the RCM Plan for further development: Brookside Elementary School,
Newell Elementary School, Iron Station Elementary School, Eastover Middle School, East Lincoln Middle School, Crest Middle School, West Lincoln
High School, and North Rowan High School.

Contents

CHAPTER 4

Implementing the RCM Plan   *109*

CHAPTER 5

Responsible Classroom Management Models   *145*

APPENDIXES

INDEX

A Comparison of School Discipline Models

To Rosemary Jocobi, the new eighth-grade social studies teacher at Washington Junior High, the early morning hall was filled with the usual noises: metal lockers slamming, friends yelling one more reminder as they ran in opposite directions, and too many feet dragging on the tiled floor. Next to her classroom, right behind the door were Lisa and Jon, whispering very seriously and holding each other, as usual. School was not their primary concern. Ms. Jocobi's greeting only lowered their whispering. Their indifference to the setting was palpable.

Placing coffee on her desk, Ms. Jocobi was pleased to see that almost everybody was seated at their assigned desks—except, of course, Lisa and Jon, still holding each other, and Janene Li and Robert, who were arguing in the back of the class. With the ringing of the bell, she expected her students' full attention. Ms. Jocobi asked Thomas, sitting next to the door, to request Lisa and Jon's presence. Tom was out of his seat before the teacher even asked; this was his usual assignment. Janene Li and Robert increased the volume of their exchange until the teacher could constrain herself no longer. She spoke to them as sternly as possible without showing her temper. She was aware that her pitch was too high for intimidation to work, but she had to gain control somehow. So the class watched nervously as she sarcastically asked the two if their marriage was faltering. The stratagem seemed to distract them. Janene Li laughed. Robert took offense and answered with a wisecrack about the teacher's ethnic group. His male friends hooted in approval.

Ms. Jocobi ignored the bait and asked the class to take out the individual assignments they had been working on for the last week. She could only hope that she had gotten on the right side of the contest by scoring a slight victory, temporary as it would be. Damon waved his hand at the teacher and asked to present his materials first. Ms. Jocobi looked around at the other hands, noting the expressions of those who did not volunteer, who were withdrawn and indifferent. She decided to ignore them; she couldn't afford to waste what little productive time she had extracting what they probably didn't know anyway.

So she quickly agreed to Damon's insistence, trying to move rapidly into the lesson without further distraction. But Robert asked, tauntingly, why he never got a chance to go first. Ms. Jocobi saw her chance to embarrass Robert and asked Damon to allow Robert to demonstrate his knowledge. Robert said that he and Janene Li had done the work together. Ms. Jocobi said she was not interested in group work. She wanted to know what he was capable of, what he had done. Robert responded with another sarcasm; this time directed at Damon. Kabir, Damon's friend, stared hard at Robert. Ms. Jocobi felt her grasp of control become increasingly precarious.

Pushing hard ahead, she proffered a short introduction, describing how she expected the class to carry on the discussion. The PA system interrupted the effort with innocuous announcements. Ms. Jocobi, clearly frustrated by the further delay, started again. The class took precious minutes to refocus. Ms. Jocobi then asked Damon to read his paper on the assigned issue of world population. She hoped the material would engage them by getting them interested in something she considered important and immediate. She knew she was taking a chance, but the topic was in the news and certainly a part of the study of world cultures. Within a few minutes, she realized she was right and wrong. The class was listening to Damon, but the class was also getting agitated as he confronted their preconceptions. Damon was being increasingly attacked for his position.

Ms. Jocobi recognized she would have to keep a tight lid on the discussion because she sensed the drift of the arguments; quite opposite to what she had hoped. These arguments were laced with threads of racial, ethnic, and class conflict. She could clearly see the ethic and racial makeup of her students; she could guess their social and economic status. But as she looked at her class more closely, she realized that she did not really know them; had not shared their experiences; did not understand the extraordinary diversity of background, ability, and interest that she confronted.

Given the perspective of a present-day classroom in the preceding vignette, in Chapter 1 we present a short analysis of the school and societal conditions that are the core of that vision. We then discuss several important discipline models that represent the spectrum of ideas that have been used by schools and teachers during the last several decades. The five approaches to controlling classroom behavior selected for review encompass a broad field of theories from the humanist to behaviorist traditions. The ideas of several psychologists and educators representing these traditions, including Thomas Gordon, Rudolf Dreikurs, Jane Nelson, William Glasser, Saul Axelrod, and Lee Canter, are introduced. Examination of these models establishes a perspective from which to view the classroom management system that is ultimately the subject of this chapter and book—Responsible Classroom Management (RCM). The RCM approach represents a broad spectrum of practical ideas and techniques, the central themes of which are personal responsibility, self-control, and intrinsic motivation.

FOR REFLECTION

What could Ms. Jocobi do with this situation to make it work? Did she have the training? Did she have the skill? Could she succeed?

CLASSROOMS AND SOCIETY

The classroom scene described previously is intended to capture a few moments of the complex dynamics and inherent potential for conflict prospering in classrooms in the United States in the late twentieth century. Undoubtedly, this image is disquieting. Social and pedagogical problems clearly abound. Examination of the classroom and the social milieu in which it operates can bring to light many of the issues confronting students and teachers.

Societal and personal conditions today are complex, difficult to grasp, and even more difficult to control. The rapidity and degree of change during the past five decades at every level of society have permeated the very institutions that have been created to provide for societal and personal growth and equilibrium. Schools are at the core of the change process and clearly manifest the character and the degree of stability of the greater society. The school and classroom are microcosms of the society and culture in which they developed.

THE SCHOOL ENVIRONMENT

Classrooms are places of social conflict, reflecting the issues of race, ethnicity, religion, and class. Given the influence of these complex issues, teachers find it difficult to model democratic procedures. To further complicate matters, teachers and others in authority often assume privileges unavailable to students. Privilege, determined by position, is often modeled in schools and classrooms.

In many classrooms, students are confronted with regimentation and predictability countered by indecisiveness and permissiveness, a confusing environment in which to learn. Although society speaks of democratic practices, multiculturalism, and children's rights, the school and teacher— the primary agents established to engender societal values—are not fully prepared to accept the responsibility of enacting these in the classroom.

For the most part, teachers do not train students to debate and follow arguments. They often do not have the time, skill, or inclination to do so, especially in light of established curricula. Knowledge of how to operate effectively in groups to achieve consensus and cooperation is often ignored. Expectations of what students should know and how they should perform are often irrelevant to the circumstances of the classroom. Teachers often present material beyond the immediate capabilities or interests of the students.

Students are expected to behave maturely and express sophisticated opinions, yet those responsible for modeling those behaviors and opinions are unaware of or insensitive to the perceptions of students and behave in ways contradictory to stated values. When teachers do not model the behavior and values that are desired, cynicism and noncompliant behavior by students can be expected.

Teachers and students compete for power and position. Teachers often use approaches to controlling students and classrooms that are unsuitable for developing mutual respect and shared responsibility. Under these conditions, authority is questioned, and the teacher's position is vulnerable to attack. The dominant approach to classroom control and discipline is haphazard, a contest of wills that is constrained by a lack of understanding of group dynamics.

Schools are often organized around an industrial model of pedagogy, a model that leaves little room for deviation from a norm of mediocrity and minimum standards. The behavior of both teachers and students is usually predictable; spontaneity is not expected to be a part of classroom life or the learning process. The instructional approach of many teachers relies heavily on individual and isolated effort, which inherently denigrates community effort and shared responsibility. It often leaves behind those without the skills and attitudes necessary to accomplish the teacher's or school's goals. Student goals are relevant only if they happen to correspond to the common matrix of effort and expectations. When students adhere to established objectives, they are good students. Students perceived as deficient are ignored, while the teacher works with productive students. In many classrooms, instruction is hurried and not organized for productive learning.

To remove these barriers to personal significance and belonging, educators must devise ways for children to develop responsibility and a mature perspective. In fact, they must help students establish a direct relationship between privilege and responsibility. The workable alternative to the current course is not unattractive; it depends on shared responsibility and is based on mutual respect, democratic values, and the recognition of humankind's claim to dignity and self-worth.

The Social Environment

The structure of American society has changed dramatically since the 1950s. The cultural changes have had a direct impact on children in school. Perhaps the most critical changes impacting education have been the changing family structure, increased violence, and an ever-present challenge to meet the needs of all students in a diverse society moving toward a global community. These challenges will be magnified to an even greater extent in the future.

The following data about changes among schoolchildren were reported in *The Challenge of Change: What the 1990 Census Tells Us About Children* (Population Reference Bureau, 1992):

- Children in 1990 composed a smaller portion of the population than in 1980, but the number of children under the age of six increased by 12.5%. In 1990, young children were as numerous as during the baby boom of the 1950s.
- School-age children from the ages of six to eleven increased by 3.4%, while the teenage group decreased by 14%.
- Non-Hispanic white children began to show a decline of 7%, as reported by the 1990 census, but they maintained the largest group, with a total of 70%.
- African American children composed the largest group of what were often referred to as "minorities" in the 1990s. This group of children totaled nearly 15% of the population. Closely following were Hispanic children, accounting for 12% of the population. Asian American and Native American children accounted for 3% and 1%, respectively.
- In 1980 African American children accounted for the majority of the minority children. The other ethnic minorities combined outnumbered the African American child population, and the traditional non-Hispanic white child population began a continuing decline.
- Nearly 20% of children lived in a single-parent environment, with by far the majority, 10.4 million, living with their mothers, and 2.0 million with their fathers.
- Of great alarm was the fact that 5.7 million children (9% of the child population) lived in a home not headed by either parent.
- From 1980 to 1990, the number of single-mother families increased by 19% and the number of single-father families increased by 68%. Among African American families, the single-parent home outnumbered the two-parent home.
- By 1990 there was a historical shift in the population, as reported by the U.S. Census Bureau. Married families with no children surpassed married families living with children.
- Children with working mothers increased by 55% in the decade from 1980 to 1990. Sixty-eight percent of women with children under the age of eighteen worked, according to the 1990 census. Sixty percent of women with children under age six worked; this was up by 60% from 1980. As children began school, the number of mothers who worked increased. Seventy-five percent of women with a child six years of age or older worked. This was an increase of 63% from 1980.
- Seventy-two percent of children lived in a traditional, two-parent home. Sixty-two percent of these children had two working parents. Of the 24% who lived with one parent, 69% of those parents were in the workforce. Sixty-four percent of all children living with a parent did not have a parent at home full-time. Nearly

10% of all children living with a parent had no working parent in the household.

There were great population increases from 1950 to 1990. According to the U.S. Bureau of the Census *Statistical Abstract of the United States* 1993 and 1955, the resident population grew from approximately 151 million to 249 million. Projections for the year 2000 are near 275 million. Campbell (1994), with the U.S. Bureau of the Census, estimates a growth of seven million students from preschool through college from 1990 to 2000.

As previously stated, some of the major changes in the family in the late twentieth century are greater poverty among children and their families, the decline of the traditional family, and the entry of a large number of women into the workforce. Additional concerns are the high rate of teenage pregnancy, school dropouts, juvenile crime, a growing rate of child abuse, and the issue of how society, especially schools, can best function in this changing environment.

In the next century, poverty and related social issues must be addressed more productively than has been the case during the twentieth century. Social programs and educational incentives must be designed and

A teacher conferences with a parent from a nontraditional home.

implemented nationwide if the educational system is to have a positive impact on poverty and related issues.

The structure and function of the American family will continue to experience significant changes. Educators must be prepared to deal with the implications of increasing divorce rates, teenage pregnancy, and violence— all of which create emotional turmoil that children carry into the class-room.

In the 1950s the American family was portrayed widely as traditional. The American dream included a father who worked outside of the home, a mother who worked as a housewife, two or three children, and home own-ership. This family was portrayed as financially comfortable, living in a world with limited poverty. As has been illustrated, much of this has changed, and more changes appear to be obvious for the future. By the late 1990s teachers will instruct children when no single set of characteristics will accurately describe the American family.

Poverty and Violence

The number of American children below the age of six living in poverty in the United States has reached an all-time high, as reported by the National Center for Children in Poverty (1995). The director of the center, Aber Lawrence, stated that a record high of six million children lived in poverty. That accounted for over one-fourth of all children below the age of six in the United States. In a period of five years, from 1987 to 1992, the number of children under the age of six living in poverty increased by one million. This continued a trend of poverty that President Johnson's War on Poverty program in the 1960s failed to reverse.

The 1990 census reflected that 18% of all children under age eighteen were poor. By the year 1992, the *Current Population Survey* (U.S. Bureau of the Census, 1992) placed the figure at 22%.

The increases as reported by the Population Reference Bureau (1992) from 1980 to 1990 demonstrate that as of 1990 more than eleven million children lived in households with incomes below the poverty level. This was an increase of 14% from the 1980 census. Within that increase, 4.3 million of these children were under the age of six, and 6.8 million were between the ages of six and seventeen. The percentage increases in children living in poverty according to race or ethnic groups in the ten-year period follow:

Non-Hispanic White	1.5%
African American	2.0%
Asian American	2.2%
Hispanic	3.1%
Native American	6.3%

Within these increases, 50% of these children lived in single-mother homes and 24% in single-father homes.

To address the social implications of future reform efforts in education, programs must confront issues of poverty and health. The U.S. Supreme Court's ruling on *Brown v. Board of Education of Topeka, Kansas* in 1954 marked the beginning of modern reform to equalize the educational opportunity of all children by outlawing segregated schools. Much of this effort was hindered by slow social acceptance and the greater impact of the Soviet launch of the spaceship *Sputnik* in 1957; while much focus was placed on science through passage of the National Defense Education Act of 1958, many schools remained poor and segregated well into the late 1960s.

The first social reform that attempted to affect education on a national level was a part of President Johnson's War on Poverty, complete with compensatory educational programs and the passage of the Civil Rights Act of 1964. Perhaps the real influence of these programs was the attention given to children of poverty. Obviously, the effects were limited. Although schools are legally desegregated, poverty, racial tensions, and violence will continue to plague the schools well into the next century.

Educators may create some of the conditions that place culturally diverse children at greater risk by not recognizing and addressing their special needs. Teachers must learn the important skill of recognizing the individuality of children and that all children must have a chance to be successful in school.

Guns and violence are major problems in society and in the schools. Education is essential to counter the widespread problem of violence. Schools must be supported by parents and the community in their efforts to change the behavior patterns of these youth by providing children with a drug-free and violence-free school environment and by training in alternatives to violence in problem resolution. According to a recent survey of seven hundred American cities conducted by the National League of Cities (Arndt, 1994), school violence in 1993 caused the death or serious injury of students in 41% of these large cities. Thirty-eight percent of the cities reported a noticeable increase in school violence over the previous five years. Seventeen percent reported that violence had gone down or was really not a problem. The rest reported that it was about the same. Counting communities of all sizes, one-fourth of the respondents reported student deaths or injuries requiring hospitalization within the previous year as a result of violence. The figures were most likely to be high in large cities: 41% for cities of 100,000 or more; 32% for cities of 50,000 to 100,000; and 19% for cities of fewer than 50,000. The largest cities also were the most likely to report increased violence over the previous five years—55% compared with 46% for the middle-sized cities and 31% for smaller communities.

Children and Education

School enrollment grew by less than 20% from 1980 to 1990, as reported by the U.S. Bureau of the Census (1992). Sixty percent of preschool students attended private schools, and 10% of elementary students attended private schools.

In 1991, 11% of all Americans ages 16 to 19 were not enrolled in school and were not high school graduates. The percentage of teens from several ethnic groups who were not attending school follow:

Non-Hispanic white	10%
African American	14%
Hispanics	22%
Asian Americans	5%
Native Americans	18%

When compared with the total population of all dropouts, whites accounted for 66%. African Americans and Hispanics accounted for 18% and 22%, respectively.

McMillen (1993), for the National Center for Education, reported a 10% reduction in the number of high school sophomores who dropped out of school between 1982 and 1992. She stated that school failure and dislike for school were the major reasons students gave for quitting school. From 1982 to 1992, 25% of female dropouts stated they left school because of pregnancy. In 1992, marriage was cited as the cause significantly less often than in 1982.

According to a study conducted for the General Accounting Office in 1993, there were about 44.4 million school-age children (ages five to seventeen) in 1990. This was a decrease from 1980. School-age children accounted for less than 19% of the total population. The increase or decrease in school-age children by race follows:

Non-Hispanic white	Decrease of 12%
African American	Decrease of 4%
Hispanic	Increase of 57%
Asian American	Increase of 87%

According to the report, by 1990, non-Hispanic white children composed less than 70% of the school-age population, down from 75% in 1980. The number of immigrant children rose by 24% during the last decade. In fact, the State of California passed a law, Proposition 187, which banned illegal aliens from attending school and receiving medical attention or any other state services, except in an emergency.

Hamburg (1992) found that, whereas adult pregnancy had declined since 1970, adolescent pregnancy had soared to one of the highest rates among the technologically advanced nations. Among his findings, teens accounted for 66% of all illegitimate births. Nearly 1.3 million children lived with teen mothers. Only 50% of these teen mothers were married. Six million children under the age of five were living with mothers who were adolescents when they gave birth. His findings verified that 20% of young American children were being raised in poverty and verified an alarming upward trend.

Rubin and Borgers (1991) found that American families have undergone profound demographic transformations and have survived as social conditions have changed. However, the educational institutions that prepare children to become capable and responsible adults have failed to keep the pace. For example, the 180-day school year with two months off in the summer was most compatible with the American lifestyle of the 1950s. However, today, family structural changes have required school boards and administrators to seriously examine such issues as magnet schools, alternative schools, and year-round schooling. Family changes have weakened the family support system essential for children's healthy development. This weakness has placed a greater burden on the schools to provide students with a stimulating and supportive environment.

In the past, society's responsibility for providing educational opportunities for children started with their entry into school. Because of the structural changes in families, schools must be restructured or re-created to respond more effectively to the ever-changing educational needs of children. Mounting societal pressures, the startling growth of the number of single-parent homes, and an increase in childhood poverty have forced public schools to assume responsibilities for the welfare of children that far exceed the traditional educational obligation. As a result, many public schools have pursued a broad social agenda and have provided a wide range of social services, including breakfast and lunch programs, health clinics, before- and after-school programs, and child care centers (Martin, 1992). Weston (1989) believes that American families must continue to play a significant role in education. Every aspect of the family—from organizational structure to value systems to the family's relationships with the rest of society—affects what a child learns. Whatever their structure, families must prepare children for formal schooling by ensuring a healthy birth and by providing the physical and emotional nurturing and intellectual stimulation necessary for successful early childhood development. Parents will be and should be their children's first and perhaps most important teachers (Martin, 1992).

FOR REFLECTION

Given the changes in society and the schools within the last 40 years, what do you predict will be the effect of those continuing trends on the schools by the year 2010?

Schools that were originally designed to educate the traditional student must now adapt the curriculum and the instructional program to the needs of an increasingly diverse population. Rich (1987) believes that changes encourage recognition of differences in racial and cultural heritage, language, health, and family situations. She encourages educators to be prepared to handle issues of family diversity with awareness, acceptance, and respect. Schools must support and assign educational roles to the family and provide families with the practical information they need to help educate their children.

Joseph (1986) suggests that teachers provide a warm atmosphere in their classrooms by allowing the children to express their feelings. She encourages teachers to become more aware of their own attitudes toward student diversity. She strongly recommends that teachers convey the attitude that there is more than one acceptable family structure.

Rubin and Borgers (1991) believe that teachers must learn greater awareness and skill in handling issues of family diversity. This should include reassurance to children that changes in families may cause feelings and emotions never previously experienced.

Today, children are subject to enormous cultural forces that neither they nor their parents understand or control. There are numerous reasons for this condition. During the last several decades, the transience of the American population has resulted, in part, in general family instability. Whatever the reasons for this dynamic, whether economic opportunity or

An example from a classroom where cultural diversity is valued.

necessity or lifestyle concerns, family members have found themselves in communities where relationships offer little support and security. This results in increased emotional strain and upheaval for the family and its individual members.

Within this milieu, it is difficult for children to develop motivation and personal responsibility. The pursuit of personal happiness and fulfill-ment, always a powerful goal in American society, has displaced the indi-vidual's obligation to the larger community and family members. One result of this isolation and separation is a dramatic increase in the number of single and divorced parents. Staying together for the "sake of the chil-dren" has become passé and, as noted previously, large numbers of children live in homes with only one natural parent. The loss in real wages during the past two decades has worsened the effects of single-parent households and resulted in highly stressed parents and children with virtually no parental guidance during a significant portion of the day. Even in homes with both parents present and substantial income, excessive television watching by all members of the family, indifferent communication, and a lack of guidance in general have increased the strain on children's appropri-ate development and maturation.

Under this divisive pressure, young people are aware of and express-ing ideas or behaviors that adults say are inappropriate. Yet adults some-times display interests and behaviors that are plainly hypocritical and that reinforce children's misbehavior. As children try to establish some basis on which to make decisions, they are constantly confronted by contradictory signals. They cannot escape the intense bombardment of estranging images; they must struggle simply to stay balanced and find personal meaning. The media regularly introduce children to ideas for which they have had little preparation. Concepts and behaviors that children in previ-ous generations would have had scant knowledge of are common fare for today's children. Complex issues and problems, normally the venue of adults, have been thrust on children indiscriminately, sometimes resulting in confusion, questioning of authority, and greater demands.

In previous generations, adults modeled obedience and submission to authority; today, this is not the case. For example, mothers work and expect equal treatment; they do not accept paternalistic authority. Gender roles are becoming less and less important in determining position and sta-tus. As parents exert independence from the old sources of authority—fam-ilies, employers, and church—they break the chain of habitual responsibil-ity and submissiveness. While gaining personal power and influence, they lose control of their children. Children's independent behavior is clearly substantiated by the home and general environment.

In the past, society often depended on authoritarian forms of control to achieve its goals; this was true in the classroom as well. Today, however, children, emulating their parents and other adults, do not respond well to this approach. They are not submissive and do not accept less than what they perceive as equal rights. Yet they are not expected to contribute significantly to the well-being of the family or the community at large. As the nation has become richer and more powerful, our children have been buried under an avalanche of material goods for which they have had virtually no responsibility to earn or to maintain. Consequently, children often become dependent by attempting to delay responsibility indefinitely and, at the same time, they demand and are willing to manipulate to get whatever it is they think they need or want. This cycle of dependence and expendability wreaks havoc on children's self-esteem and ultimately leads to irresponsible behavior.

All of these demands on family life and on children in particular have diminished the ability of children to accommodate the schools' and society's social and academic demands. As children are forced to achieve more socially and academically at increasingly earlier ages—a clear contradiction of the real status of children in this society—adult authority will be questioned to an even greater degree.

THE DISCIPLINE MODELS: HUMANISTS TO BEHAVIORISTS

Since the 1960s, as many of the previously mentioned problems have been considered, educators and researchers have developed several approaches to dealing with what they considered the primary issue—school discipline. These approaches represent a broad spectrum of philosophical and psychological ideas and techniques, ranging from the humanistic and student-centered to the behavioristic and teacher-centered.

The humanistic, student-centered approaches are primarily concerned with the inner self and its needs and capacities. The developers of these approaches and theories, including the psychologists and educators Carl Rogers (1972), Abraham Maslow (1970), and Thomas Gordon (1974), believe that the inhibition of the rational thought process diminishes the ability of children to behave within acceptable limits. The procedures generated by this group are used to remove the obstructions to the rational thought process and to enhance children's understanding of their own behaviors. This group rejects the use of any kind of reward system as manipulative and unwholesome to child development.

At the spectrum's center and humanistic in their approaches, psychologists and educators Mortimer Adler (1990), Rudolf Dreikurs (Dreikurs, Grunwald, & Pepper, 1982), Jane Nelson (1987), and William Glasser (1969) express concern for children's natural propensities for rational thought and social interaction. Their positions are activist oriented. Each author has developed prescriptive and interventionist means to assist children in gaining control of their behavior. This realm of thought and practice requires children to respond to and alter their behavior but, never-theless, continues to count children's inherent propensities as the founda-tion on which to establish acceptable behavior.

On the behaviorist, teacher-centered end of the spectrum, educators and psychologists such as B. F. Skinner (1982), Saul Axelrod (1977), and Lee Canter (Canter & Canter, 1985) have developed ideas and strategies that are designed to directly control children's behavior through manipula-tion of external rewards and, in one case, the application of punishment. The goal, or end product, of the behavioral approach is to structure chil-dren's behavior according to defined expectations. The psychological causes of children's behavior are irrelevant to the undertaking. Reference to the inner child of rational thought and higher needs is not useful to this approach.

Later in this chapter, we present the principles of Responsible Class-room Management (RCM) in the context of this review of discipline mod-els. The relationship of RCM to the approaches representing the spec-trum's center are evident throughout the discussion. The review and analysis begin with the humanist, student-centered approaches, proceed to the teacher-centered behaviorists, and are followed by a discussion of RCM. Figure 1–1 summarizes the five discipline models discussed in this chapter.

Teacher Effectiveness Model

Thomas Gordon's Teacher Effectiveness Training (TET) model (1974) reflects the theories of Abraham Maslow and Carl Rogers. According to these theorists, obstructing children's drive to achieve growth by ignoring their rational selves and forcing children to behave in a certain way are the bases of misbehavior. The uniqueness of the individual makes it impossible to appropriately direct another person. It is important that children build self-confidence in their ability to make decisions and solve problems; whether a solution is correct or not is less important. To accomplish these goals, the interrelatedness of student and teacher must be recognized and accommodated by both parties. Gordon says,

> The relationship between a teacher and a student is good when it has (1) Openness or transparency, so each is able to risk directness and honesty with the other; (2) Caring, when each knows that he is valued by the other; (3) Interdependence (as opposed to dependency) of one on the other; (4) Separateness, to allow each to grow and to develop his uniqueness, creativity, and individuality; (5) Mutual Needs Meeting, so that neither's needs are met at the expense of the other's needs. (1974, p. 24)

In TET (Gordon, 1974), the teacher's role is to facilitate the develop-ment of the child's capacity for rational analysis and for solving life's prob-lems. Teachers should avoid exerting control through questions and direc-

FIGURE 1-1
Five Discipline Models: Major Points

	Student Centered Discipline Models			Teacher Centered Discipline Models	
	Thomas Gordon **Teacher Effectiveness Training**	Rudolf Dreikurs **Positive Discipline**	William Glasser **Reality Model**	Saul Axelrod and B. F. Skinner **Behavior Modification**	Lee and Marilyn Canter **Assertive Discipline**
Principles	Children strive for growth through the rational self; obstructing this pursuit causes misbehavior. Children cannot be directed, because they are unique.	Children strive to overcome a sense of inferiority by establishing a unique set of goals. Children primarily strive to belong. Children must experience the consequences of their behavior.	Children must learn to acknowledge irresponsible behavior and to accept the consequences. Children must take steps to behave logically and productively.	The inner rational self is a myth. Environmental stimuli determine behavior. Children work to avoid negative experiences and seek pleasant ones.	Children respond to conflict passively, hostilely, or assertively. Teachers have a right to teach and to meet their own basic needs. Teachers have a right to assert maximum control over student discipline.
Goals	Build self-confidence to make decisions and solve problems. Support children's capacity for rational analysis.	Instruct children on how to belong. Help children develop a sense of compassion and community spirit. Help children understand the value of equal rights and human dignity.	Children will learn to make judgments about behavior and will commit to change based on rational analysis. Children will not avoid responsibility for behavior.	Teachers can control classroom environment and student behavior to achieve learning objectives. Children's behavior can be modified to acceptable standards.	Establish a classroom environment that provides an optimal learning environment. Meet teacher needs while encouraging social and educational development of the child.

Strategies	Teacher pursues open communications. Children must identify and take ownership of problems. Children learn to actively listen. Children use Dewey's scientific method.	Teachers determine which goals are motivating students' behavior through observation or questions. Teachers use encouragement and natural and logical consequences.	Teachers demarcate parameters of acceptable behavior. Teachers must focus children's attention on undesirable behavior so they consider rationality of behavior. Teachers develop behavior contract/plan with students.	Teachers can evaluate and alter elements of classroom environment to affect a child's behavior. Teachers often use four intermittent reinforcement schedules. Teachers can use contingency contracting.	Teachers verbally limit student misbehavior. Teachers signal correct course of behavior. Teachers are assertive in their demands and never negotiate. Teachers use limit-setting consequences. Teachers develop a plan for discipline.
Problems	Differences in children's growth and development make implementation difficult. Rationality and language abilities diminish the ability of children to deal with problems. Children have difficulty with complex reasoning operations.	It is very difficult to determine which goals are motivating student's behavior. Children often send false or mixed signals. Aggressive or violent children are difficult to deal with. It is difficult to differentiate between punishment and logical consequences.	This approach relies on an extraordinary degree of teacher patience. Children's physical or psychological difficulties may be beyond teachers' ability to use this approach effectively. Children may not be capable of devising a meaningful plan to improve their behavior.	Behaviorism is manipulative and treats students undemocratically. This system controls behavior without developing rational capacity. This system removes emotions and eliminates choice and the development of problem-solving strategies.	This approach establishes an authoritarian classroom environment. Students' rights are minimized. The responsibility of students to develop self-control is removed. The common discipline plan not useful within a group. This approach ignores individual differences.

tives while trying to understand students. Instead, they should encourage students to examine their feelings in a nonjudgmental manner in pursuit of rational understanding of the troublesome behavior.

To accomplish these objectives, the teacher must pursue unaffected and open communications. Gordon (1974) offers passive listening, acknowledgment responses, door openers, and active listening as means to open communications. Active listening represents an important use of open communications in the Gordon model. Gordon states that active listening can be used to promote inquiry, to establish an environment in which children will express ideas, and, in general, to facilitate learning. The process of active listening requires a teacher to summarize for students the problems and feelings that they are communicating to the teacher. Through this process, the teacher lets students know that they are understood. However, TET directs the teacher not to provide a direct solution to the problem once it has been clarified. To offer solutions and directly advise the student would set up roadblocks to the student's understanding, a negation of the fundamental principles of Gordon's program.

The primary issue, once the problem has been identified, is to determine who owns the problem. In Gordon's (1974) view, a teacher owns the problem when the student's behavior is having a direct effect on the teacher's behavior, and, alternatively, the student owns the problem when the student is having a problem. The teacher's role in the first instance is to use an "I" message that describes the behavior, the effect the behavior is having on the teacher, and the feelings the teacher is having as a result of the student's behavior. On close analysis, it is clear that some problems do not have a direct impact on a teacher and may be the result of value conflicts or teacher prejudices. "I" statements in these instances do not work. When a student owns a problem, the teacher should use door openers and critical and active listening to assist the student in clarifying the problem.

In Gordon's (1974) view, classroom conflict resolution is contingent on the type and use of authority in the classroom. In what Gordon describes as type 1 authority, teachers depend on personal strengths, including knowledge, experience, and expertise, to exercise authority. Type 2 authority, however, relies on the power role of teachers. In this role, teachers provide rewards and punishments to achieve control. Gordon sees positive and negative reinforcement as highly manipulative and undesirable, resulting in defensive responses by students.

In conflicts between teachers and students in which behavior inhibits the satisfaction of either the students' or teachers' needs, Gordon (1974) suggests that teachers often use one of two methods to solve a problem, moving between the two approaches as the situations change. Reflecting the authoritarian classroom, teachers use position and power to control and win. Alternatively, in the permissive classroom, students win because the teachers express indifference or give up in the face of confrontation. These zero sum games, where the winner takes all, are self-defeating and destructive to students and teachers.

To achieve his goals, Gordon (1974) offers a third approach, which relies on problem solving, active listening, and "I" messages. This win–win approach requires that both parties work together until a satisfactory solution to the problem is achieved. To facilitate this proactive process, Gordon suggests that teachers use Dewey's six-step scientific method, which consists of defining the problem and generating, selecting, implementing, and evaluating possible solutions. This rational process underlies TET's goals. The behavior exhibited by teachers using method 3 models the values essential to developing self-directed students.

Finally, TET is concerned with establishing a classroom environment that strongly supports student growth and development. Accordingly, space, time, and learning activities should be managed to maximize learning and creativity and to minimize disruptions (Gordon, 1974).

Several questions and problems have arisen regarding the implementation of TET. Certainly, students differ intellectually and emotionally. They develop at different rates and to different degrees. The rationality and the language abilities of students at different stages of development vary, diminishing the degree to which teachers can effectively work with students. According to cognitive psychologists such as David Ausubel (1986), younger children do not respond to hints effectively, and they cannot generalize problem solutions to different or remote situations. They also have difficulty with complex reasoning operations, especially those involving two or more isolated experiences. But even for those children who are verbally sophisticated, the ability to verbally express emotions accurately may be quite limited. In younger children, the ability to distinguish between external reality and internal, subjective experience is substantially less than in older children. In fact, adequate rationality may be achieved only in adolescence.

Additionally, a major concern for many teachers is that it may be unreasonable to expect twenty to thirty students to maintain self-control and stay on task as they carefully apply TET methodology to individual students. This is an especially important question when the student is being disruptive or even violent. These conditions complicate the time-consuming process of problem identification and solution and limit the effectiveness of TET procedures.

Positive Discipline Model

In the humanist tradition, the works on classroom discipline of Rudolf Dreikurs (Dreikurs, et al., 1982) and disciple Jane Nelson (1987) are based on the theories of Austrian psychiatrist and educator Alfred Adler, who believed that children strive from early life, within a social context, to overcome a sense of inferiority by establishing a unique set of goals and means for achieving them. Adler used the term *style of life* to describe this pursuit.

This behavior is primarily oriented toward achieving goals, most importantly the goal of belonging. Often, however, children make serious

errors in determining how to achieve their goals and act in ways that actually contradict fulfillment of their desires. Accordingly, misbehavior reflects
children's misconstruence about how to achieve primary goals, the most
important of which is belonging (Dreikurs et al., 1982). Within this context, the teacher must teach children how to belong. Children must also
learn compassion and how to contribute to the community in which they
live. They must be taught to value equal rights and the dignity of all
human beings (Nelson, 1987). These authors reject any approach to disci-
plining children that fails to develop belongingness, equality, and mutual
respect.

> We do not regard the child as the victim of forces that converge on him:
> hereditary, talent, or environmental influences, traumatic experiences,
> psychosexual development, and so on. What he is when he is born is
> less important than what he does with it afterwards. The living condi-
> tions in which he finds himself are less important than what he does
> with himself in those conditions. This view opens the way for change
> through new and appropriate concepts and goals. It is the basis for a
> more optimistic outlook. (Dreikurs et al., 1982, p. 5)

Dreikurs's (Dreikurs et al., 1982) and Nelson's (1987) discipline
schemes assume that misbehavior is the result of the drive to satisfy four
subconscious and inappropriate goals: getting attention, power and control,
revenge, and helplessness or inadequacy. Within the context of adolescence,
peer approval and the pursuit of excitement are also mistaken goals. The
initial phase of Dreikurs's methodology and Nelson's follow-up work in
establishing belonging and acceptable behavior is to determine which of
these goals is motivating the student's behavior.

To accomplish this objective, teachers should observe students in various situations and then hypothesize about which goal motivates the undesirable behavior. Teachers should evaluate their feelings in conjunction
with each of the four goals. According to Dreikurs (Dreikurs et al., 1982)
and Nelson (1987), understanding personal feelings in relation to a student's behavior will help determine the goal a student is trying to achieve.
Nelson suggests that if the goal is attention, then the teacher's response
may be irritation or annoyance. When the goal is power and control, she
says that feeling threatened may be the response. If revenge is suspected,
hurt may be the response. Finally, in the case of helplessness, the likely
response is a feeling of inadequacy in meeting the needs of the child.

Teachers can further substantiate their understanding of a student's
goals by asking direct disclosure questions. For example, teachers may ask,
"Is it possible that you want special attention?" A simple yes or no may
disclose the goal. Or, a student's "recognition reflex" such as a smile, a
laugh, or an unexpected movement may provide the information (Dreikurs
et al., 1982). During the questioning, it is particularly important to remain
calm and objective and not provide the means by which children can

achieve the inappropriate goal. Once the goal has been identified, teachers can work to replace the inappropriate goal with the preferential goals of equality and mutual respect. Regarding teenagers, Nelson (1987) insists that teachers will achieve cooperation only when mutual respect and equality are applied to solving problems.

Dreikurs (Dreikurs et al., 1982) offers several possible teacher responses to children's misdirected efforts. In the case of attention getting, teachers should not give attention when children are demanding it; rather, teachers should attend to students in an effective manner after deciding it is appropriate to do so. For example, children may be permitted to tell a story to the class at a special time established for such things, thereby satisfying their needs for special attention in an appropriate way. When power and control are the underlying goals, teachers might appoint students as hall monitor or line leader. These are appropriate uses of power. The misdirected goal of revenge requires teachers to apply compassion where it may be difficult to do so. Frequently expressing concern and affection to students may ultimately deter students from acting out hostility to gain revenge. The most discouraged children are those who display the fourth goal, helplessness. Helplessness results from overambitiousness, competition, pressure, or failure. For these students, teachers must be extremely patient, help them to understand what is happening, and constantly lead them into successful work experiences.

Dreikurs et al. (1982) and Nelson (1987) reject the use of punishment and positive and negative reinforcement. Even praise, a form of positive reinforcement, is discarded as inappropriate because it creates dependency. The use of punishment, according to Nelson, only serves to discourage children and provoke them to focus on anger and revenge and not on the behavior that caused the punishment in the first place. Accordingly, punishment may actually reinforce uncooperative behavior and alienation.

Fundamental to positive discipline is the use of encouragement and natural and logical consequences. According to Dreikurs et al. (1982) and Nelson (1987), teachers should use encouragement to elicit mutual respect and optimism where conflict and confrontation may have previously existed. Encouragement is a process by which students are permitted to experience success at each stage of improvement. The use of encouragement disallows criticism of students; only students' actions are criticized. In addition, competitive conditions are avoided, and mutually supportive situations are arranged by teachers.

To learn responsibility, which is fundamental to a democratic society, children must experience the consequences of behavior (Dreikurs et al., 1982). By doing so, they can develop an understanding of what effects their actions have on themselves and on the community in which they are acting. Natural consequences occur directly as a result of an act, such as going outside in the rain without an umbrella and getting wet, whereas a logical consequence is arranged by teachers and has an inherently logical connection to the behavior. For example, a student failed to respond to roll call for several days. The teacher, knowing the child was present, decided not to read the student's name the next time he called roll. The student reacted immediately and henceforth desisted from ignoring roll call.

The effectiveness of a logical consequence on students' behavior is determined by the degree to which a teacher successfully clarifies the relationship of a specific student misbehavior to the applied consequence and the time when it is used. When attention is the goal of the student's behavior, immediate use of logical consequences is effective. However, when power or revenge is the purpose, teachers should permit a cooling-off period before using logical consequences. In the case of helplessness, Nelson (1987) advises against the use of consequences.

To ensure that a consequence is logical and not a punishment, Nelson (1987) applies the standards of relatedness, respectfulness, and reasonableness to the potential consequence. Importantly, teachers' rational and calm use of consequences counters the way students see punishment, as a vengeful act in controlling their behavior. The use of isolation (easily seen as punishment by students) to ameliorate the conditions of behavior is an acceptable strategy if the criteria for logical consequences are met. While using isolation, teachers should use encouragement to assure children that they are welcome back to the classroom whenever they feel in control of their behavior.

Dreikurs et al. (1982) and Nelson (1987) believe that classroom meetings are a powerful means of expressing the values and techniques used in the positive approach to discipline. Dreikurs believes that schools are laboratories for the development of children's capacity for democratic action and ideals. Both educators suggest that regular class meetings be used to discuss problems and policies and to model democratic processes. Accordingly, the effects of successful meetings are manifold. Nelson suggests that through the use of problem-solving techniques children will learn cooperation, responsibility, mutual respect, and interest in social issues. In addition, listening, language and memory skills, the capacity for extended and objective thinking, the ability to understand the consequences of behavior, and appreciation for the value of learning will be improved.

Nelson (1987) also suggests that children can improve problem-solving abilities, build greater responsibility, and develop leadership abilities through peer counseling. This process requires that selected children, who are willing to do peer counseling, be trained in a five-step procedure intended to guide the peer counselors in defining and solving a fellow student's behavioral problem.

Numerous concerns about the positive approach to discipline have been raised by critics and practitioners. Foremost is the issue of determining the underlying goal of a child's behavior. Within the context of a busy classroom, is it realistic to analyze every student's misbehavior to determine the motivating force? In the case of an aggressive or violent student, is it possible to apply this strategy? Some children will give false signals or no discernible signals at all. What should teachers do in those cases? Certainly, Nelson (1987) assumes that children want to know and understand their own behavior. In most instances, that is probably the case, but some students will be fearful and resent the effort to clarify incorrect behavior and will fight teachers' invasive attempts to understand them.

Some critics view attention and the use of consequences and encouragement as contrary to Dreikurs's (Dreikurs et al., 1982) and Nelson's (1987) rejection of praise and other forms of positive reinforcement. The difference between a logical consequence and a punishment is very thin and potentially problematic. Also, the constant use of encouragement for minor improvements strengthens children's acceptance of less than what they are capable of attaining. The importance of high achievement, for example, is therefore weakened. Finally, there is concern that classroom meetings may actually put unneeded stress on certain students who do not have the communication skills or emotional maturity to participate effectively in the meeting. How do teachers deal with such complex circumstances?

Reality Model

Psychiatrist William Glasser (1990), creator of reality therapy, bases his approach to behavior control on the idea that people must learn to acknowledge their irresponsible behavior and take the steps necessary to behave in a more logical and productive manner. Glasser rejects ideas that require analysis of the unconscious and those that nonjudgmentally accept an individual's behavior while searching for a rational explanation of the offending behavior. Rather, he believes that people must learn to accept the consequences of their actions, regardless of claims to psychological inadequacy, and must learn to live in the world responsibly without infringing on the rights of others. In *Reality Therapy*, Glasser says:

> Responsibility, a concept basic to Reality Therapy, is defined as the ability to fulfill one's needs, and to do so in a way that does not deprive others of the ability to fulfill their needs. . . . A responsible person also does that which gives him a feeling of self-worth and a feeling that he is worthwhile to others. He is motivated to strive and perhaps endure privation to attain self-worth. When a responsible man says he will perform a job for us, he will try to accomplish what was asked, both for us and so that he may gain a measure of self-worth for himself. (1990, p. xi)

Fundamental to Glasser's (1990) approach is the notion that children have certain needs that must be met either by the home or by the school. When students behave inappropriately, the cause, according to Glasser, is that their basic needs are not being met. If the home does not satisfy those needs, then the school must try to meet them. Accordingly, the school and teachers must assist children in succeeding in what they undertake, in their effort to learn, and in their pursuit of self-worth. It follows that if children misbehave in school, then teachers must somehow help them to meet unmet needs. If children cannot adjust and make their behavior more productive, then teachers must find ways to alter their own behavior or the structure and contents of the classroom.

Glasser (1990) also insists that teachers should not try to alter children's environment to allow them to avoid the consequences of behavior. Changing the school environment is not the same as altering rules and expectations so that children can avoid injury to their self-worth. Rather, teachers should help students make value judgments about what is causing a problem. When children make judgments about their misbehavior and commit themselves to change, they will learn responsibility. And once children commit to change, teachers can accept no excuse for failure to maintain the commitment.

With these ideas in mind, it follows that to guide student behavior, Glasser (1990) would expect a teacher to establish clearly demarcated parameters of acceptable behavior. He recommends that teachers confront unacceptable behavior forthrightly by describing it and then following with strong statements and commands that describe the desired behavior.

The issue for teachers is children's misbehavior. Therefore, teachers must focus the children's attention so that the children will discontinue the undesirable behavior and act acceptably. Often, children will not cooperate immediately and must be further convinced to behave appropriately. To accomplish this, Glasser (1990) suggests that teachers formulate questions to direct students to consider the rationality of the offending behavior. Children are then expected to describe the misbehavior. The objective of teacher questions is not an explanation or an excuse for the behavior but rather is a clear statement from students about what is happening.

Allowing children to explain an inappropriate behavior merely serves to provide a means by which children can avoid responsibility for the problem. Keeping children focused on the issue will permit teachers to affect an immediate alteration in behavior. Because the underlying concern in reality therapy (Glasser, 1990) is to develop responsibility for personal behavior, teachers must urge offending students to plan alternate and desirable behavior.

Essential to Glasser's (1990) approach is ensuring that children are not permitted to escape responsibility for misbehavior. This does not mean that teachers should punish or praise children for some act. The effect of punishment and praise is to disconnect children from directly accepting responsibility for the undesirable act. Punishment also permits children to focus on the punishment and the consequent feelings of revenge. Praise motivates children to seek ways of extending praise to any and all activity, thereby delaying development of self-motivation. As an alternative, Glasser believes that teachers should use logical consequences to develop responsibility.

Glasser (1990) recommends that teachers develop a contract between students and teachers to guide student behavior. The students' signed plan or contract should include a clear statement as to what the consequences will be for not adhering to the behavioral agreement. The critical issue in developing a plan is to identify a privilege or activity that is clearly more valued by students than the offending behavior. For some children, this will certainly be more difficult, but Glasser insists that it is generally possible to achieve.

The use of time-out or isolation as a deterrent to misbehavior can be viewed as a form of punishment; however, in Glasser's (1969) scheme, isolation is used as a logical consequence of misbehavior. Glasser uses isolation as an opportunity for misbehaving children to rectify their behavior. During isolation, according to Glasser's view, recalcitrant children should consider their behavior and plan what must be done to return to the classroom. When the behavior does not improve, Glasser suggests suspension from school, which he considers the most drastic form of isolation. Again, students may return after they prepare a plan for behavioral improvement. An important issue here is that teachers must remain positive and helpful throughout the periods of isolation. The teacher's role during isolation is to uninhibitively inform students of their offending behavior, either directly or through pointed questions, and to foster students' willingness to develop a plan for improvement.

Central to Glasser's (1969) approach to discipline is the use of class meetings, of which he designates three types: social problem solving, open ended, and educational diagnostic. Glasser recommends that teachers use meetings to assist students in recognizing their place in and responsibility to the group and to sort out interests and problems in the curriculum and the instructional approach. Glasser indicates that it is important to carefully maintain control of a meeting when a child's behavior is the subject of discussion because of the possibility of destructive results. Within this context, students learn to define a problem, propose solutions, and construct plans for change.

More specifically, teachers use problem-solving meetings to solve individual and group educational problems. Any problem relevant to the school, classroom, or an individual is subject to consideration. The primary concerns of teachers are to act nonjudgmentally, to help participants to solve problems, and to avoid accusations and retribution. The open-ended class meeting is used to examine any area of concern to students. To Glasser (1969), the open-ended meeting is critical to making education relevant. In an educational-diagnostic meeting, the teacher and students examine the subject in which the class is involved to determine the effectiveness of instructional procedures.

Glasser's (1990) approach to classroom discipline has several substantial problems. The approach relies on what seems to be an endless degree of teacher forbearance and optimism. It appears that the approach is not based on a realistic understanding of teaching or the time available to teachers to carry out their instructional responsibilities. There are clearly instances when the resources necessary to deal with a problem are unavailable. Sometimes a teacher may lack interest or skill. At other times, the complexity of the child's psychological or physical condition may intervene in achieving a productive outcome. Certainly, there are children not particularly susceptible to the threat of isolation. The constant application of questions, from teacher to student during isolation, requires a time commitment that may not be justifiable or achievable.

An important step in Glasser's (1990) approach is that students develop a plan for behavioral improvement. Students clearly vary in their thought and language capabilities. What constitutes an effective plan for a student who has limited capacity to develop one? Finally, classroom meetings are difficult to operate and control and are beyond the capacity of school organizations to sustain, especially at the middle and secondary levels. The outcomes of these meetings are not always favorable to a student's well-being. And, does a meeting have the potential of giving too much power to children who are unaware of the larger issues and too unsophisticated to make decisions about other children and about instructional and curriculum matters?

Behavior Modification Model

The behaviorist movement began as a result of Russian physiologist Ivan Pavlov's stimulus–response experiments in the early twentieth century. He believed that habits and higher mental activities were determined by chains of conditioned reflexes. Later, experimental psychologists and educators such as Saul Axelrod (1977) and B. F. Skinner (1968, 1982) further explored and then applied stimulus-response theory to the human condition in general and to schooling in particular.

To behaviorists, the inner rational self is a myth. Rather, environmental stimuli determine human behavior and can be modified to shape behavior to acceptable social standards. A fundamental principle underpinning behaviorist thought is that people work to avoid painful or unpleasant experiences or stimuli and seek those that are pleasant and rewarding. Within the context of the classroom, students cannot be expected to derive solutions to problems based on their rational understanding of their inner selves. Instead, the teacher must evaluate how each of the elements of the classroom environment is affecting student behavior and alter those elements to affect acceptable behavior.

Modifying the behavior of students within the classroom environment requires the use of what behaviorists call *reinforcers*, which are categorized as positive or negative. *Positive reinforcers* refer to desirable stimuli that, when offered to a person, strengthen and increase the behavior they follow. Behaviorists generally offer several different terms to describe positive reinforcement, including primary or unconditioned, social, and conditioned, including token reinforcement.

Teachers use primary reinforcement when they use items that satisfy basic biological needs, such as providing popcorn or candy to positively reinforce an appropriate behavior (Axelrod, 1977). In an example of primary reinforcement, students receive cookies for standing quietly in line for a specified period. The desired behavior, standing in line, is strengthened and can be expected to be displayed more readily. When teachers praise or approve certain behaviors or give attention to students when they perform appropriately, they are using social reinforcement. When reinforcing acceptable student behavior with items exchangeable for desirable stimuli such as privileges, activities, or events, teachers are using token reinforcement. Successfully arranging rewards, or contingencies as they are called by behaviorists, to increase acceptable behavior is said to actually condition or shape student behavior.

Keller (1969) states that negative reinforcers, as opposed to positive reinforcers, strengthen behavior when the stimuli are removed. Negative reinforcement is used, for example, when a teacher offers to eliminate a final exam if students pass all the quizzes during the term. In this instance, the undesirable event—the final test—will remain in place until the desired behavior is achieved. Generally, students will act in ways that minimize undesirable events when negative reinforcers are applied, but they may not alter their behavior permanently once the reinforcer is discontinued.

Teachers often confuse the use of punishment with the use of negative reinforcement. According to behaviorists such as Axelrod (1977), punishment will decrease unacceptable behavior for an uncertain period of time but will not increase acceptable behavior. In fact, punishment will sometimes reinforce the inappropriate behavior teachers want to extinguish.

A benefit cited by classroom behaviorists (Axelrod, 1977) is that teachers can control this system more exactly than other systems of discipline because they can apply contingencies based on a precise reading of student behavior. In a correctly planned and implemented behavior modification program, teachers observe student behavior and establish a baseline. After applying reinforcing contingencies, teachers measure the change in behavior and then reverse the procedure to double-check the effect of the reward or contingency. This system clarifies cause and effect and removes much guesswork in classroom discipline efforts.

Behaviorists (Axelrod, 1977) often use four intermittent reinforcement schedules—fixed interval, variable interval, fixed ratio, and variable ratio—to achieve their ends because these schedules generally reflect real-life situations better than regular schedules. Each of these schedules has particular advantages and disadvantages, but the underlying purposes of each schedule are to reward desirable behavior often and to lessen the amount of reinforcement as the desirable behavior is expressed.

An especially effective technique used by behaviorists (Axelrod, 1977) to teach a new or terminal behavior is called *shaping*. Shaping behavior requires teachers to deconstruct gross behaviors into smaller and simpler components, which can then be modified through the reinforcement schedules. This procedure requires teachers to prioritize the increments of behavior and treat them one at a time until the terminal behavior is achieved.

In the initial application of a behavior modification plan, Axelrod (1977) notes, teachers usually ignore student misbehaviors and apply subtle social reinforcers, such as smiling or winking, when acceptable behavior is observed. Often, however, teachers are frustrated during this period because students respond by significantly increasing their unacceptable behavior. But, as teachers consistently apply the strategy of ignoring the undesirable behavior and reinforcing the desired one, the undesired behavior will likely be extinguished.

Students do not always respond as teachers expect, and for various reasons students sometimes must be physically removed from the reinforcing environment of the classroom and placed in a nonreinforcing environment, called by behaviorists a *time-out area*. Time-out areas are used to isolate students from reinforcing stimuli. The period of isolation is specified at the time of intervention. An alternative to isolation is satiation. Satiation may be used to eliminate particularly difficult behaviors that have not responded to normal reinforcement schedules. Satiation requires students to repeat a reinforcing but unacceptable behavior until they are unwilling to continue doing so and the behavior is extinguished. In an example of satiation, children are forced to chew several sticks of gum until it becomes unmanageable, and the unacceptable behavior is discontinued.

Axelrod (1977) reports that another important technique in the behaviorist's repertoire is the use of *modeling* or imitation. Modeling is useful in teaching specific behaviors and is considered especially useful when teachers must deal with disruptive students and must convey appropriate behavior. Teachers can use student peers and adults important to the disruptive student's particular interests as models. A student observed to be group leader may be an ideal candidate for modeling, if the leader's behavior can be made to reflect acceptable behavior.

Within the behaviorist model, language is valuable as a reinforcer and as the means of communicating behavior modification plans to students, as in the case of contingency contracts. Behaviorists suggest that teachers use language as a positive reinforcer when they observe students acting unacceptably, directing students to the appropriate behavior. When teachers use positive language to direct students, they broaden the students' knowledge of acceptable social behavior. Critical or demeaning language punishes students and, as do all types of punishment, does nothing to clarify students' understanding of acceptable behavior.

Axelrod (1977) states that teachers can apply behavior modification procedures to the classroom through contingency contracting. This involves the development of a behavioral contract between student and teacher. The two parties determine the amount of an acceptable behavior or task that must be demonstrated and the amount of reinforcement that will be provided. Using guidelines developed by Homme (1969), a teacher can develop a contract with a student. The contract should be precisely stated in terms of student and teacher expectations. Contracts should be established for individuals rather than for groups because of differences in developmental levels and learning rates. The student–teacher agreement should call for frequent incremental rewards for small and incremental improvements in behavior rather than large rewards for large behavioral improvements. The reward should be immediate and frequent, especially at the beginning, when students are becoming familiar with the process. The contracts should call for tasks achievable within an established time frame; and the expected reward should be balanced against the significance of change in behavior.

Criticism of the behavioral model is concerned with several issues. From the humanist tradition comes the concern that behaviorists treat children in an undemocratic and manipulative manner. Controlling behavior without developing a child's rational capacity is unacceptable in a society that professes humanistic principles and depends on independent, ethically evolved people.

In the cognitive realm, minimizing mental operations by obviating emotions and eliminating choice and the development of problem-solving strategies will harm intellectual development. At a more mundane level, critics note the system's complexity, mechanistic approach, and the excessive time the system requires for record keeping, planning, behavioral analysis, and the application of reinforcement procedures.

Assertive Discipline Model

Another behavioral approach, and one that has been used extensively during the past several years, is Lee and Marlene Canter's assertive discipline model (1985). The Canters developed assertive discipline based on assertion training, which assumes that people respond to conflict in basically one of three ways: passively, hostilely, or, the preferred approach, assertively. Accordingly, assertive discipline teachers are not highly aggressive or overzealous; rather, their behavior is based on the right of a teacher to teach and to meet basic needs. On this basis, the teacher asserts maximum control over student discipline within the classroom environment. In

conjunction with this principle, the Canters affirm that teachers possess
the following rights inherent in their position as teachers:

1. The right to establish a classroom structure and routine that provides the optimal learning environment in light of your own strengths and weaknesses.
2. The right to determine and request appropriate behavior from the students which meet your needs and encourage the positive social and educational development of the child.
3. The right to ask for the help from parents, the principal, etc., when you need assistance with a child. (1985, p. 2)

Fundamental to the model (Canter & Canter, 1985) is the notion that teachers must treat students alike, applying the same standards and expectations for success to all students. Teachers should not discriminate based on their assumptions about a student's condition. These negative expectations are roadblocks that inhibit teachers from dealing effectively with classroom behavior. As a result, roadblocks also curtail the development of successful classroom discipline behavior on the part of the teacher and student. The Canters cite eight general areas that cause teachers to react to a child presumptively: emotional illness, heredity, brain damage, ignorance, peer pressure, inadequate parenting, socioeconomic background, and classroom environment.

According to the model (Canter & Canter, 1985), when students resort to undesirable activity, teachers have several options for verbally limiting misbehavior before inaugurating punishing actions. Initially, teachers can send a subtle message or hint to all students in the classroom. This approach attempts to signal the offending student about the correct course of behavior without singling out and embarrassing that student. If this approach is unsuccessful, teachers can then direct a question to the recalcitrant student, providing implicit direction without confrontation. Teachers use the third verbal limit once the first two verbal engagements clearly have failed. The third verbal limit, or "I" message, is inherently confrontational, directing students to behave in a specific manner. When this is unsuccessful, teachers then proceed to establish the fourth verbal limit, stating unequivocally what will happen if students do not comply with the teacher's wishes immediately.

Within this context, the teacher's mode of presentation is important. Eye contact, hand gestures, using names, and touching are cited as important elements in setting verbal limits. Accordingly, teachers must exhibit assertive behavior when speaking to students. To convey resolve, teachers must not retreat or lose emotional control; they should directly face an offending student, identify the student by name, and use expressive hand movements and a low and controlled voice. It is also productive, according to the Canters (1985), to stare steadily at the student to make the teacher's intentions clear.

Importantly, the Canters (1985) insist that teachers should not make a demand without being certain that they will actually carry out the stated consequence if the students do not meet the demand. But to minimize conflict, teachers present each demand as a choice between what they desire and what the student had previously agreed to and the consequence to the student for not concurring. As a result, when students misbehave, they have decided by choice to accept the negative consequences of the action.

To achieve the objectives of assertive discipline, the Canters (1985) believe that teachers should purposefully adhere to a demand and never negotiate with noncomplying students. Teachers should use the broken record method of constant repetition to focus student attention on the misbehavior and on the behavior that is being demanded. As a consequence of using this method, teachers can calmly focus on personal and professional wants and needs rather than on the manipulations of students. Of course, teachers must pay careful attention to immediate circumstances that might make it impossible for a student to comply with a teacher's wishes.

The Canters (1985) use limit-setting consequences including time-out, removal of a privilege or positive activity, detention, use of the principal's office or the student's home for isolation, time-out in another classroom, tape recording, and systematic exclusion to deal with difficult behavioral problems. For students who regularly behave unacceptably, the Canters recommend isolation in an environment that is nonsupportive of the misbehavior. The principal's office, an alternative classroom, or even the student's home with parental assistance are regarded as acceptable isolation areas.

Within the scheme of assertive discipline, the Canters (1985) recommend that teachers use positive assertions to reinforce desirable behavior. The behavioral plan should include the means to regularly reward students for acceptable behavior. This might include positive notes or phone calls to parents, awards, special privileges, or even special material consequences. They further recommend that teachers use a contract as a useful method of implementing follow-through consequences. The contract should be designed to deliver a positive reinforcement quickly, it should be flexible, and it should include limit-setting consequences. An example of a contract is, "If you sit in your seat quietly for thirty minutes, I will give you ten extra minutes to read a book of your choice."

The assertive approach (Canter & Canter, 1985) to control classroom behavior relies heavily on the development of a plan for discipline. To establish a discipline plan, teachers determine what behaviors they will eliminate or accept, what positive and negative consequences will be attached to the behaviors, and what planning should be accomplished to implement the consequences. The plan includes rules that the teacher thinks are important to effective classroom operation. Teachers state the rules precisely, avoiding general statements that can be too easily misinterpreted. Importantly, teachers must determine what actions they will consistently take to reinforce those students who behave appropriately. According to the Canters, teachers should discuss and file the discipline plan with the principle for approval and safekeeping.

The Canters (1985) believe that teachers can assertively control the classroom more effectively if they carefully prepare themselves before presenting the plan to students. To achieve the correct degree of assertiveness and confidence, teachers should practice explaining the various segments of the plan in the same manner they will present it to students. Once teachers feel self-assured and certain of their ideas, they can then present the plan, discuss the contents, and have the students sign a copy to indicate their understanding. Within the model, success is contingent on the degree to which teachers can convince students of their seriousness and the rightness of their position.

Several issues have been raised regarding the assertive approach to discipline. The Canters' approach establishes an authoritarian environment in which students have virtually no rights and are mere recipients of teachers' demands. The centrality of teachers' needs and demands in this model denies the inherent dynamic and reciprocal nature of human interaction. Thus, student responsibility to develop self-control, awareness of the self as part of a larger group, and the capacity for consensus building, which are the basis of the democratic classroom, are lacking in the Canter model.

Within the assertive classroom, the development of a common discipline plan for all students and the unidirectional mode of communication—teacher to student—forces teachers to ignore individual differences and to potentially act in ways irrelevant to the particular needs of a classroom. This position contradicts those who believe that teachers must assist students in developing their inner rationality and personal standards of behavior and fulfill their basic physical, psychological, and social needs. By approaching students assertively, without concern for students' developing self-reliance and rational decision making, teachers fail to educate students according to democratic ideals.

Finally, the Canters' use of limit-setting consequences contradicts research findings that show reinforcement schedules work to increase or decrease specific behaviors; however, though punishment may diminish undesirable behavior temporarily, it does not work effectively over the long term and may actually reinforce the misbehavior.

THE RESPONSIBLE CLASSROOM MANAGEMENT MODEL

Responsible Classroom Management (RCM) is rooted in the thinking of humanist psychologists Abraham Maslow and Mortimer Adler and cognitive developmentalists such as Erik Erikson, Richard Havighurst, Lawrence

Kohlberg, and Jean Piaget. Based on this foundation, RCM shares many ideas with the programs of Dreikurs (Dreikurs et al., 1982), Nelson (1987), and Glasser (1990).

RCM is based on the theory that every child moves through several common developmental stages. These stages determine, to a high degree, the behaviors, attitudes, cognitive capabilities, and physical characteristics that a child will exhibit at any particular time. These proclivities, in combination with interactions with parents, siblings, peers, and teachers, greatly influence the pattern of behavior that a child adopts. To ensure that children grow and prosper and develop into healthy and well-balanced adults, adults need to provide every child with unconditional love, security, and the certainty of belonging.

Fundamental to children's well-being is the ability to find workable solutions to life's problems. Within a hierarchy of learned behavior, the RCM model supports the development of a capacity to solve problems. Children must be taught to examine and solve the many social and academic problems that they will encounter during their growth. Accordingly, they must be given the opportunity to creatively and independently explore the world, define and achieve goals, and feel success on which they will build self-assuredness, self-esteem and, ultimately, a strong self-concept.

RCM assumes that most children, even so-called problem or dysfunctional children, can be taught to behave responsibly in the classroom, in school, and in the community at large by competent and responsible adults, regardless of a child's socioeconomic or family history. Behaving responsibly, according to RCM, means in part acting in accordance with an internalized set of values and beliefs and with acceptance of the consequences of an act, whether positive or negative. On a continuum conveying degrees of responsible behavior, students who are responsible most often self-correct behavior, use an internal locus of control, accept the consequences of their behavior, and follow guidelines to a greater degree than students who are less responsible. But regardless of where they fall on the continuum, most students can be taught to behave responsibly.

Close analysis of almost any classroom will reveal that approximately 88% of the students never require disciplinary actions by teachers. Though teachers might have to restate expectations, these children generally behave acceptably. Within the same classroom, approximately 12% of the students will, however, require varying degrees of attention. Most of these children are attention seekers or extremely active and require some corrective measures. Usually, in these cases, teachers succeed in controlling these misbehaviors by being constantly vigilant and regularly interacting. However, the real challenge lies in dealing with those one or two students in most classrooms who exhibit anger, aggression, and mistrust in their behavior and attitudes. Their noncompliant behavior can be highly disruptive and require exceptional treatment to make the classroom a viable operation.

Problem students often share certain commonalties. Many of these students have been abused or mistreated by primary caregivers, including parents and former teachers. Although it is true that a significant portion of these students learn to conform or become withdrawn, some children will exhibit aggression and hostility. The behavior of this small group of children can have a disproportional effect on the general behavior of the entire class. The undesirable behavior of a single child can rapidly and insidiously ripple through a class with devastating effect. The RCM program is structured to avoid this situation and to encompass the needs of many of these students.

Children accept the values and emulate the behavior of people, such as teachers, who are important in their lives. As responsible adults, teachers must consciously model values, attitudes, and behaviors that will lead children to behave responsibly. Adults who are irresponsible model irresponsible behavior and often make decisions detrimental to themselves, as well as to children who depend on them for guidance. To be effective, positive models, RCM teachers must be responsible adults. Responsible and competent teachers understand and skillfully practice the principles of child growth and development and carefully monitor the quality of their own actions in guiding a child to responsible behavior.

An underlying problem in today's culture is that parents and teachers fear that they might damage a child's self-esteem merely by correcting unacceptable behavior. When children express dismay because their demands have not been met, attending adults often respond with feelings of guilt. Rather than expect a change in the children's behavior, adults alter their own behavior to avoid the children's unhappiness. In behaving in this manner, adults are acting irresponsibly. By being overly concerned with the children's happiness, adults forget the more important issue of providing guidance.

Guidance is essential to the development of responsible children. Adults use guidance when they point in the direction of the desired behavior. When adults model what is defined as important and desirable to the community, they guide children in becoming successful members of that community. Importantly, guidance does not preclude children from experiencing the consequences of exploration into acceptable and unacceptable behavior. By learning through honest mistakes and sometimes difficult experiences, children will learn responsibility. By permitting children to safely experience the natural consequences of behavior, parents and teachers guide children appropriately and responsibly. By contrast, the use of authoritarian or permissive forms of control often incites children to be uncooperative and belligerent and, most critically, gives them little opportunity to internalize appropriate behavior. When blind obedience and control or indifference are demanded, responsibility and self-control are non-issues.

An important goal of the RCM approach to classroom management is to develop responsible children who can live productively in a democratic and multicultural society. Within the RCM classroom, responsibility is taught and then expected. Teachers and the school organization must implement democratic principles in teaching and leadership roles. The concepts of human equality, dignity and self-worth, participation in decision making at all levels, and acceptance of the consequences of behavior must be integrated into the curriculum and consistently taught.

The school and classroom environment and the concomitant instructional effort are central to the RCM approach. In an environment that is safe and inviting, children will feel secure and protected and will be prepared to learn. The more positive the experience of the classroom, the greater the opportunity that teachers will have to guide students toward responsible behavior. In an environmentally sound and attractive school and classroom, the organization of space and time, the organization and presentation of instructional materials, the demeanor of the teachers, and the amount and kind of preparation are each critically important to success.

The RCM approach to instruction requires teachers to clearly state the objectives of all planned classroom activity. This outcome-based approach to instruction necessitates careful preparation and constant evaluation of student behavior by teachers. Precise and sensitive instructional guidance builds the foundation for responsible student behavior. When teachers involve students in a dynamic agenda, replete with value and purpose, students will respond with certainty and optimism. As students are encouraged to perform at higher levels within the context of the RCM classroom, they will not feel threatened but, rather, will feel motivated to meet their own standards. RCM teachers encourage, and indeed acknowledge, exceptional performance and responsibility, but do not fall prey to the use of rewards and other forms of bribery to sustain responsible students. The goal of RCM teachers is to avoid external rewards as a means to motivating student learning. Responsible students are intrinsically motivated students.

External rewards are often the primary means by which teachers attempt to motivate students to learn and behave acceptably in the classroom. This process is time-consuming and often results in children who rely solely on extrinsic rewards to accomplish what should be intrinsically important to them. In contrast to this scheme, the RCM approach to classroom management uses high expectations and reasonable guidelines and standards to develop intrinsic motivation. Within the context of the RCM classroom, teachers act swiftly, consistently, and unemotionally in effecting desirable behavior. As students learn to internalize responsible behavior, their self-esteem matures, and they gain increasing control over their behavior.

In many classrooms, teachers create strict and inflexible rules of behavior which, by their very nature, force students to misbehave. The RCM plan of classroom management does not require teachers to monitor students for conformance to a code of discipline for which they have no responsibility and little understanding. Instead, RCM teachers teach students to follow socially acceptable standards and guidelines that students participate in developing.

Within the RCM classroom, children are considered individuals who must be treated fairly and equally, but not necessarily the same. Strict use of rules to obtain obedience serves to insulate students from personal responsibility, a result contrary to RCM goals. When children are taught to act autonomously according to agreed on standards, they will act responsibly. Responsible behavior does not require enforcement and will likely be repeated without the application of external inducements. Accepting the premise that most children are naturally very honest, fair, and willing to cooperate, RCM teachers use natural and logical consequences to teach children to self-correct behavior. Forcing children to behave in a certain way is wholly unnecessary when children have internalized the standards of behavior and have become responsible. In learning to act responsibly, children learn to be productive members of the community. As a result, responsible children are not discipline problems.

The RCM plan defines a classroom management system that is designed to teach students acceptable guidelines and standards for their behavior. RCM allows administrators to monitor and guide students in nurturing and accountable ways. It gives teachers the independence to develop productive and stimulating classroom strategies to assist students in controlling their personal behavior. With the RCM plan, students are motivated to take an active role in developing and implementing classroom learning experiences. As children take responsibility and are held accountable for their learning and self-discipline, they prepare for their future as mature and actively engaged adults.

Issues Affecting the Implementation of RCM

It is particularly difficult to prescribe who should be in any classroom. Clearly, it is impossible to predict that only one or two students in any classroom will be dysfunctional. It is also true that the complexity of a child's background may be such as to be beyond the skills of the classroom teacher and require a specialist to treat the child's problems. Of course, teachers must be skilled and self-assured to a degree that will permit them to recognize and properly deal with situations beyond their expertise. In some instances, even only moderately problematic children will cause serious difficulties for unprepared teachers. When even one child is particularly difficult and disruptive, unskilled teachers may lose an entire class because of the chaos generated.

In a less serious situation, it is not unusual to observe teachers who ignore those students who have adjusted their behavior by withdrawing from normal interactions but cause little classroom upheaval. These students are acting out their frustrations in a manner that they have found successful, but the indifferent teacher is ultimately acting irresponsibly by leaving well enough alone.

Children's behavior is not always predictable and is subject to alteration when family, school, or social conditions change. Even responsible children may exhibit irresponsible behavior at times; teachers are responsible for skillfully guiding children to responsible behavior. If teachers' expectations are unrealistic or poorly defined and, therefore, fail to provide realistic markers for responsible behavior, a child or even an entire classroom of children may suffer academically and behaviorally and become a problem.

For the sake of order, predictability, and satisfying the needs of the greatest number, teachers may sometimes rely on formulaic approaches to instruction. These approaches to teaching are detrimental to the development of children's sense of responsibility. Creativity, exploration, problem solving, and independent action are limited, resulting in bored and alienated students who seek stimulation through alternate and often undesirable means. By approaching instruction in a bland and uninvestigative manner, teachers deny a fundamental principle of RCM and, more importantly, the dictates of human growth and development.

A phenomenon evident in the general culture and in many classrooms is the apparent contradiction between stated values and beliefs and personal behavior. This is as true of teachers and administrators as it is for the general population. Often, classrooms are anything but democratic in organization or operation. Though it is certain that children do not have the knowledge and skills necessary to guide themselves through the complex web of academic and social problems they will be confronted with during their development, it is critical that they be given every opportunity to explore and confirm the superiority of the values they are told are important and, indeed, fundamental to their way of life.

In some classrooms, value conflicts may emerge that are inherently disruptive. Unprepared teachers will often exacerbate conflict and actually contradict the goals of RCM. Without understanding a child's values, it may be impossible to successfully pursue these goals. Multicultural conflicts between middle-class teachers and inner-city students, representing various ethnic and racial groups, require special attention. If teachers are not knowledgeable about and sensitive to value conflicts, classroom interactions will remain shallow and unproductive and, possibly, adversarial. The use of guidelines, standards, and consequences by teachers in culturally divergent classrooms may be irrelevant if teachers apply a personal perspective without resolving underlying conflicts. Mutual understanding and appreciation must be pursued consciously. Differences and commonalties must be examined and prejudices put aside through conscious effort.

To succeed, RCM teachers must analyze their own behavior to determine where they might inject unfavorable behaviors and attitudes into the classroom. Tendencies toward authoritarian or permissive control, prejudice, ignorance of the correct methodology, indecisiveness, uncertainty about the goals of RCM, or simply laziness will each undermine the RCM classroom.

The use of external rewards in the form of reinforcement schedules and even the casual use of praise are each, according to the RCM view, detrimental to the development of responsible children. The use of these techniques verifies the contrived and irrelevant nature of the classrooms in which they appear. In a dynamic, creative, and uncontrived classroom, teachers depend on the excitement that results from tapping a child's inherent need to know, to learn, and, very importantly, to belong. RCM teachers derive a significant portion of stability in classroom behavior from the excellence of their instructional preparation and execution. The use of standards and guidelines and natural and logical consequences is carefully entwined into the instructional process by successful RCM teachers.

The previous discussion described the basic characteristics and rationale of RCM and issues potentially affecting the implementation of the program. In the remaining chapters, a discussion of child growth and development and the specific components and methods that schools and teachers should use to implement RCM are presented in detail.

A teacher contacts a parent to request assistance and support.

Putting Concepts into Practice

The RCM Plan Inventory

The purpose of the inventory in Figure 1–2 is to assist you in clarifying your professional knowledge and attitudes about the underlying principles of RCM. The task requires a simple response, from *agree* to *disagree*, with *uncertain* as an uncommitted response. After completing the instrument, you can compare your responses to the ideal responses that are suggested. Strong general agreement on the items suggests that you understand and agree with the fundamental principles and practices of RCM. A strong general disagreement signals either misunderstanding or rejection of RCM. An uncertain response indicates that you are unclear about RCM, the meaning of a particular statement, or your own values and practices. By examining your responses, you can determine areas of concern and further explore the underpinnings of RCM. Before attempting to implement a program such as RCM, it is critical that potential users understand and agree with the principles that will be put into practice.

FIGURE 1–2
The RCM Plan Inventory

Response Items	Agree	Uncertain	Disagree
1. Children and adults move through common developmental stages that affect their behavior.			
2. Teachers should ignore student misbehaviors and smile or wink when acceptable behavior is observed.			
3. Children should be taught problem-solving methods.			
4. Self-assuredness, self-esteem, and a strong self-concept are fundamental to success in school.			
5. Problem or dysfunctional children cannot learn responsibility and should be separated from normal children.			
6. A poor socioeconomic and family history make it impossible for a child to learn responsible behavior.			
7. Children should rely on extrinsic motivation to control their behavior.			
8. Teachers should reinforce acceptable student behavior with items exchangeable for privileges, fun activities, and events.			
9. Responsible children self-correct their behavior, use an internal locus of control, and accept the consequences of their behavior.			
10. Teachers should reward students immediately and frequently, especially at the beginning, when students are becoming familiar with correct behavior.			
11. Only a small number of children in almost any classroom require serious attention for misbehavior.			
12. It is important for teachers to model appropriate values and behavior.			
13. Teachers should use positive and negative reinforcers to modify the behavior of students within the classroom environment.			

Response Items	Agree	Uncertain	Disagree
14. Teachers should carefully monitor their own behavior in the classroom.			
15. Teachers should avoid correcting misbehaving children to avoid damage to the children's self-esteem.			
16. When children express dismay because they have been denied the satisfaction of a demand, teachers should change their own behavior to meet the needs of the children.			
17. Teachers' guidance precludes children from experiencing the consequences of their behavior.			
18. Children should be allowed to experience the natural consequences of their behavior.			
19. An authoritarian approach to discipline permits children to develop an internal locus of control.			
20. Teachers should not be concerned with developing democratic and multicultural values.			
21. The concepts of human equality, dignity, self-worth, and participation in decision making at all levels should be taught by teachers and integrated into the curriculum.			
22. The school and classroom environment are not important to developing responsible students.			
23. A safe and inviting classroom is irrelevant to children's success in school.			
24. Teachers should clearly state the objectives of instruction.			
25. Teachers should praise children for exceptional performance.			
26. Teachers should not punish children for misbehavior.			
27. Punishment and consequences are not the same.			
28. Teachers' use of encouragement or praise will have the same positive effects on children's attitudes and behavior.			
29. Responsible children rely solely on external rewards to motivate learning.			

FIGURE 1–2, *continued*

Response Items	Agree	Uncertain	Disagree
30. External rewards are essential tools in controlling student behavior.			
31. Teachers should not rely on strict rules to control children's behavior.			
32. Expressing strong emotions when dealing with children's classroom misbehavior is effective in controlling that behavior.			
33. Teachers should closely monitor students for conformance to a code of discipline.			
34. Children should be involved in the development of behavioral standards and guidelines.			
35. Teachers should eliminate negative consequences so that children enjoy school.			
36. Children should question the rules established by teachers or school.			
37. Within the context of the classroom, students cannot be expected to derive solutions to problems based on their rational understanding of their inner selves.			
38. Responsible behavior must be constantly reinforced with external inducements.			
39. Responsible children have internalized acceptable standards of behavior.			
40. Forcing children to behave allows children to internalize acceptable standards of behavior.			
41. Children usually are unwilling to cooperate unless forced to do so.			
42. Students should take an active role in developing and implementing classroom learning experiences.			
43. The inner rational self is a myth.			
44. Students should be taught to act autonomously.			
45. Teacher demeanor has substantial effects on children's behavior in the classroom.			

Response Items	Agree	Uncertain	Disagree
46. Teachers should not use popcorn, candy, or other enjoyable items to positively reinforce an appropriate behavior.			
47. Children should be permitted to experience the consequences of their behavior.			
48. Teachers should arrange rewards to increase acceptable behavior.			
49. When children are treated equally, they are always treated fairly.			
50. Teachers should reward desirable behavior often and lessen the rewards as the desirable behavior is expressed.			
51. Children require a sense of security and belonging to function in school effectively.			
52. As a result of their misbehavior, students must sometimes be physically removed from the classroom environment and placed in a time-out area.			
53. To control behavior, teachers should direct students to repeat an unacceptable behavior until the students are unwilling to continue doing so.			
54. Teachers should provide incremental rewards for small and incremental improvements in behavior.			
55. Most children do not require strong disciplinary actions in the classroom.			

Key to RCM Plan Inventory

Agree: 1, 3, 4, 9, 11, 12, 14, 18, 21, 24, 26, 27, 31, 34, 36, 39, 42, 44, 45, 46, 47, 51, 52, 55

Disagree: 2, 5, 6, 7, 8, 10, 13, 15, 16, 17, 19, 20, 22, 23, 25, 28, 29, 30, 32, 33, 35, 37, 38, 40, 41, 43, 48, 49, 50, 53, 54

REFERENCES

Adler, M. J. (1990). *Reforming education: The opening of the American mind.* New York: Collier Books.

Arndt, R. C. (1994). *School violence in American cities: NLC survey overview.* National League of Cities: Washington, DC.

Ausubel, D. P. (1986). *Educational psychology: A cognitive view.* Boston: Werbel and Peck.

Axelrod, S. (1977). *Behavior modification for the classroom teacher.* New York: McGraw-Hill.

Campbell, P. R. (1994). *Population projections for states by age, race, and sex 1993 to 2020.* U.S. Bureau of the Census. Washington, DC: U.S. Government Printing Office.

Canter, L., & Canter, M. (1985). *Assertive discipline.* Santa Monica, CA: Canter and Associates.

Dreikurs, R., Grunwald, B. B., & Pepper, F. C. (1982). *Maintaining sanity in the classroom* (2nd ed.). New York: Harper & Row.

General Accounting Office. (1993). *U.S. Bureau of the Census.* Washington, DC: U.S. Government Printing Office.

Glasser, W. (1969). *Schools without failure.* New York: Harper & Row.

Glasser, W. (1990). *Reality therapy.* New York: Harper & Row.

Gordon, T. (1974). *T.E.T. Teacher effectiveness training.* New York: Peter H. Wyden.

Hamburg, D. A. (1992). *Today's children: Creating a future for a generation in crisis.* New York: Times Books.

Homme, L. (1969). *Use contingency contracting in the classroom.* Champaign, IL: Research Press.

Joseph, P. B. (1986). The changing American family. *Social Education, 50*(6), 458–463.

Keller, F. (1969). *Learning: reinforcement theory.* New York: Random House.

Martin, J. R. (1992). *The schoolhome: Rethinking schools for changing families.* Cambridge, MA: Harvard University Press.

Maslow, A. H. (1970). *Motivation and personality* (2nd ed.). New York: Harper & Row.

McMillan, M., et al. (1993). Dropout rates in the United States, 1993. MPR Associates. U.S. Government Printing Office: Washington, DC.

National Center for Children in Poverty. (1995). *National Center for Children in Poverty: A program report on the first five years.* New York: Columbia University School of Public Health.

Nelson, J. (1987). *Positive discipline.* New York: Ballantine Books.

Population Reference Bureau for the Center for the Study of Social Policy. (1992). *Challenge of change: What the 1990 census tells us about children.* Washington, DC: Author.

Rich, D. (1987). *Schools and families: Issues and actions.* Washington, DC: National Education Association.

Rogers, C. R. (1972). *On becoming a person.* New York: Houghton-Mifflin.

Rubin, L., & Borgers, S. B. (1991). The changing family: Implications for education. *Principal, 71*(1), 11–13.

Skinner, B. F. (1968). *The technology of teaching.* New York: Appleton-Century-Crofts.

Skinner, B. F. (1982). *Skinner for the classroom.* Champaign, IL: Research Press.

U.S. Bureau of the Census. (1955). *Statistical abstract of the United States: 1955.* Washington, DC: U.S. Government Printing Office.

U.S. Bureau of the Census. (1992). *Current population survey.* Washington, DC: U.S. Government Printing Office.

U.S. Bureau of the Census. (1993). *Statistical abstract of the United States: 1993.* Washington, DC: U.S. Government Printing Office.

Weston, W. J. (1989). *Education and the American family: A research synthesis.* New York: New York University Press.

SUGGESTED READINGS

Evertson, C. M., Emmer, E. T., & Clements, B. S., et al. (1989). *Classroom management for elementary teachers.* Upper Saddle River, NJ: Prentice Hall.

Froyen, L. A. (1993). *Classroom management.* Upper Saddle River, NJ: Merrill/Prentice Hall.

Glasser, W. (1986). *Control theory in the classroom.* New York: Harper & Row.

Purkey, W., & Strahan, D. (1989). *Positive discipline: a pocketful of ideas.* Columbus, OH: National Middle School Association.

Ross, D. D., & Bondy, E. (1993). Classroom management for responsible citizenship: Practical strategies for teachers. *Social Education, 57*(6), 326–328.

Sacher, S. F. (1992). *From homes to classrooms to workrooms: State initiatives to meet the needs of the changing American family.* Washington, DC: National Governors Association.

Tauber, R. T. (1995). *Classroom management: theory and practice.* New York: Harcourt Brace.

Developmental Aspects of Growth and Behavior

In Chapter 2 we examine the growth and development of children from their preschool years to late adolescence. We take a developmentalist position in these areas, believing that children move from an immature and less complex and skilled dependent state to a mature and more complex and skilled independent condition. The process, as we see it, involves a series of invariant stages of physical, intellectual, and personal development. We discuss the theories of Jean Piaget, Erik Erikson, and Lawrence Kohlberg in support of this position.

To effectively implement the Responsible Classroom Management (RCM) program, teachers should understand the fundamental principles of child growth and development. By understanding the stages of development that children invariably move through, teachers will know what to expect of children, what and how to instruct, and how to communicate with children at various times in their development. Without this knowledge, effective instruction and classroom control cannot be reliably achieved. Teacher competence in these areas relates directly to effective implementation of RCM.

We begin this discussion with a presentation of the salient physical characteristics that children exhibit as they develop from birth through adolescence. As their bodies mature, children manifest significant changes in their intellectual and psychological capacities. To understand these changes, we examine Piaget's theory of cognitive development. We then describe Erikson's ideas concerning personality development. Finally, we discuss Kohlberg's conception of moral consciousness. The interrelationship of these theories will become evident as they are presented.

The usefulness of human developmental theories to RCM educators is based on the principle that children are highly dynamic and extremely sensitive to the total environment in which they live and learn. Furthermore, the complexity of the maturation processes that children undergo requires that adults and, specifically, teachers implement instructional and management strategies suitable to the individual child's intellectual and psychological condition. When teachers act without regard for or even acknowledgment of children's capacities, teachers will fail to teach, and children will fail to learn. Positive classroom discipline will likely not be reflected in those classrooms.

FOR REFLECTION

Think back to your childhood. As you read Chapter 2, identify trends in your life that illustrate significant characteristics of each theorist's stages of development.

When teachers understand and implement effective instructional strategies based on a clear understanding of child development, the foundation of effective classroom discipline will have been established. An effective classroom management system grows out of an effective instructional system and becomes positively reciprocal with it. Effective use of RCM procedures ultimately signifies the suitability of the underlying instructional system. RCM procedures based on a solid foundation of instruction will succeed when they are employed by skillful teachers.

PHYSICAL DEVELOPMENT FROM EARLY CHILDHOOD THROUGH ADOLESCENCE

Human development is a complex and ongoing process that commences with the fertilization of a female's egg by a male's sperm and the formation of a zygote. Within these cells resides the genetic material which, in combination with the intrauterine and extrauterine environments, provides the basis for the future development of the physical, intellectual, and personal characteristics of each human being. Each of these elements should be viewed as integral to the overall growth process. Though we discuss the physical, intellectual, and personal characteristics separately, they are separated only for purposes of analysis. The discussion begins with a depiction of the physical characteristics of young children.

Very young children are marked by a high center of gravity, the head being somewhat out of proportion to the size and weight of the body. A protruding abdomen further diminishes balance. As they develop, their legs and torsos begin to grow more rapidly, distributing their weight more evenly and permitting more balanced locomotion. The most significant physical achievement of preschool children is their increased control over fine and gross motor activity. During this time, they also begin to favor the right or left side of the body. This may be observed during play or during such activities as coloring. With improved dexterity and precision, children learn to perform such fine motor activities as tying shoelaces and printing letters of the alphabet. Their ability to jump, run, and walk also improves significantly by the end of the preschool period.

By the time most children reach school age, they have already learned numerous additional skills, including buttoning and zipping pants and jackets, buckling belts, cutting with scissors, and coloring within predetermined borders. Additionally, children will print letters and words with greater accuracy. After the seventh year, most children continuously improve the quality of their fine and gross motor skills, introducing few entirely new basic capabilities.

Through the primary years, children experience comparatively small alterations in their weight and height. Until children reach age nine, boys are generally only slightly heavier and taller than girls. From their eighth through tenth birthdays, both sexes are very similar in size. But by their tenth year, girls outdistance boys in weight and height. During the early elementary years, children require frequent exercise to accommodate skeletal growth and muscular development. Although most children have already learned such skills as running, jumping, and throwing, they will improve these skills through frequent practice. By their ninth year, children's improved balance, eyesight, and dexterity permit them to engage in complex activities, such as playing musical instruments, or constructing complicated models, such as a multipiece plastic spacecraft.

Fourth-grade, nine-year-old children are generally stronger and healthier than younger children. With added energy and continuous activity, their coordination shows substantial improvement over those only a year younger. Though boys and girls are similar in size at the beginning of fourth grade, by the end of the year many girls will have begun to gain height and weight over boys. They will maintain this advantage until the eleventh or twelfth year, when boys begin their major growth period.

The rapid growth of limbs and the slower development of the torso experienced by girls at this time causes them to appear ungainly and to loose a degree of strength and coordination. This diminished condition is only temporary, however. Most early maturing females rapidly regain lost ground. By the end of fifth grade or the beginning of sixth grade, they are generally taller and heavier than most boys of the same age. By this point, many girls will have reached the size they will retain until puberty.

With the onset of female menstruation at approximately age thirteen and male ejaculation between thirteen and sixteen years, girls and boys enter puberty. Changes to the body as a child moves through puberty to mature reproductive capability are substantial. The sequence of these changes is most often the same for each person, but the rate at which females and males mature may vary widely. Some people may mature fully in as little as eighteen months from onset; whereas others may require five or six years. During this period, almost every organ and system in the body is subject to change and stress.

The differences between prepubescent and postpubescent adolescents are significant. The appearance of both males and females is altered considerably by changes in primary and secondary sexual characteristics. Height, muscular development, amount and location of hair, and body proportions are each altered during this period. Significantly, early and late onset of puberty in either sex places additional stress on the person experiencing it. For those who experience puberty early, the notoriety caused by their advanced development is confusing and generally unwelcome. But as they successfully work through these changes, awkward self-consciousness diminishes and confidence improves. When a person undergoes these changes particularly late, up to six years later than the earliest, even greater difficulty may be experienced. An apparent lack of physical maturity, especially in males, may cause self-doubt, loss of self-esteem, and withdrawal from involvement with others. Some of these problems may carry over into adulthood.

COGNITIVE GROWTH

Subsequent to John Dewey's formation of the developmentalist approach to educational psychology in the first half of the twentieth century, insight into the progressive nature of child development was most notably achieved by Arnold Gesell. Gesell (1948/1971) established a center for research into child development at Yale University, where he promulgated the notion that children's growth and development occur in an unvarying sequence within strict temporal boundaries. Though his ideas were later found to be inadequate in explaining the true nature of development, his fundamental principle that children move through several phases of reorganization during which they construct new ways of perceiving the world has been generally accepted.

As Gesell worked at Yale, psychologist and epistemologist Jean Piaget (1954) quietly explored the intellectual development of his children in Switzerland. His discoveries and the work that followed have become the basis of cognitive science in the fields of psychology and education. Piaget concluded that cognitive growth occurs in specific developmental stages, during which significant differences in the nature and substance of intelligence are manifested over time. Piaget saw these differences as qualitative in nature, real transformations of consciousness.

Based on his extensive observations, Piaget (1954) defined several stages of cognitive development. He described from three to six stages of development with several substages. In this discussion, we refer to the four stages of cognitive development shown in Table 2–1.

Piaget (1954) established a general time frame for the onset of particular stages (see Table 2–1). From birth to two years of age, a child is in the sensorimotor stage of development. The period of preoperational thought is active from the second year until approximately the seventh year. This is followed by the stage of concrete operations, which generally appears by the age of seven and continues through the eleventh year. The onset of formal operations, the fourth stage, occurs sometime between the eleventh and sixteenth birthdays.

Piaget (1954) determined that the onset of each stage is signaled by a major shift in intellectual activity from the preceding stage of development. Though the commencement of each stage varies for each individual, the sequence of the stages is invariable. Children must navigate through the succession of stages; they cannot intentionally avoid or miss a stage through superior cognitive attributes. Piaget noted that although definable

TABLE 2–1
Characteristics of Piaget's Stages of Cognitive Development

Cognitive Stages	Ages	Characteristics
Formal operations	11 to adulthood	Cognitive structures mature to the adult level; capacity to engage all categories and classes of problems, the verbal abstraction, the hypothetical, and consideration of past and future conditions; ability to evaluate a logical argument separate from its content.
Concrete operations	7–11 years	Logically examine the observable relationships among events, objects, and people; development of the cognitive structures of seriation and classification; express a strong tendency to organize and apply strict rules to activities undertaken.
Preoperational	2–7 years	Not restricted to immediate environment; expand use of mental images; expand application and understanding of vocabulary; intuitive thought defines preoperational thought.
Sensorimotor	Birth to 2 years	Period of simple reflexes; restricted to immediate experience; experience events uninhibitively through sight and feeling; build first cognitive structures.

intellectual activities describe each period, mixing of capabilities from other stages, especially those from previously experienced stages, will occur. In addition, as children age there is an increasing variation in the age at which they begin a stage. The onset of formal operations in adolescents is subject to the greatest age variation. But before examining the four stages of development further, we discuss the ideas that describe the cognitive processes responsible for the changes within those stages.

Schemata and the Process of Assimilation, Accommodation, and Equilibration

In Piaget's (Piaget & Inhelder, 1969) scheme of cognitive development, assimilation and accommodation are the means by which children integrate new experiences into cognitive structures called *schemata,* or *schemes*. According to Piaget, "A scheme is the structure or organization of actions as they are transferred or generalized by repetition in similar or analogous circumstances" (Piaget & Inhelder, 1969, p. 4). These structures develop from birth, when they are simple and undifferentiating. As a child develops and is better able to differentiate between stimuli, the number of schemata increases and grows by absorbing additional relevant material that resulted from encounters with the environment. At major periods of transformation, such as when children move from the sensorimotor to the preoperational stage, schemata undergo significant alterations that permit children to deal competently with more complex problems.

Assimilation and accommodation compose an unending process that reflects a person's continuous interaction with an almost infinite number of stimuli, "a constant filtering of input and modification of internal schemes to fit reality" (Piaget & Inhelder, 1969, p. 6). During a given stage of development, schemata expand as they encounter stimuli that fit into recognizable patterns permitted by the structure. A change in the schemata may occur, however, when children cannot assimilate an experience into the established structure. If the experience cannot be assimilated, then two alternatives are available to children: The old insufficient schemata can be adjusted to accommodate the new material, or a completely new structure can be established to accommodate the material.

The process of assimilation and accommodation (Piaget & Inhelder, 1969) is the basis for cognitive growth and development that occurs throughout the individual's life. Yet the process would be unworkable if the comparative quantities of assimilation and accommodation were not balanced. A person who assimilates everything would have too few schemata and be unable to differentiate experiences. Alternatively, a person who accommodates experiences excessively would have too many schemata and would find too few commonalties to generalize to the broader world of experience. This balancing process is called *equilibration*. It is a process to which the engaging intellect is constantly drawn. Equilibrium must be sustained if the intellect is to develop effectively.

Sensorimotor Period

From birth through two years of age, children move through what Piaget (Piaget & Inhelder, 1969) has called the sensorimotor period, which consists of six substages. During this period, children move from a period of simple reflexes to one when representation of unseen objects readily occurs. Within these first two years, children are restricted to immediate experience. Without any previous experience, children of this age group have no basis on which to build categories for organizing reality; rather, they experience events uninhibitively through sight and feeling. This directness of the experience can be said to be intense, with nothing separating the child from the environment. Learning, of course, is equally intense.

One of the most important events that stage-1 children experience during the early months of life is the constant appearance and disappearance of familiar objects. From this activity, children build cognitive structures, such as object permanence, which are essential to continued mental development. Piaget says that during the sensorimotor period

> The system of sensori-motor schemes of assimilation culminates in a kind of logic of action involving the establishment of relationships and correspondences and classification of schemes; in short, structures of ordering and assembling that constitute a substructure for the future operations of thought. But sensori-motor intelligence has an equally important result as regards the structuring of the subject's universe, however limited it may be at this practical level. It organizes reality by constructing the broad categories of action which are the schemes of the permanent object, space, time, and causality, substructures of the notions that will later correspond to them. (Piaget & Inhelder, 1969, p. 13)

Restricting or denying children strong visual experiences during this period may cause deficits in the development of important cognitive structures. An environment filled with a variety of visual and reacting stimuli will provide the most supportive conditions for developing children's intellectual capabilities. An environment devoid of appropriate stimuli may result in serious delays in children's cognitive development that may not be easily rectified.

Period of Preoperational Thought

The second stage of children's development is called the *period of preoperational thought* (Piaget & Inhelder, 1969). To enter this stage, children undergo a major intellectual transformation. No longer restricted to their immediate environment, children expand on the use of mental images they began to develop during the previous stage. They rapidly extend their capacity to store information, such as words and the implicit rules of language. During this period, children's application and understanding of vocabulary increase substantially. At two years of age, the average child can use a few hundred words; whereas, by the age of five, the same child may be using more than two thousand words. This major advance in language capability is a mark of this period of intellectual development.

According to Piaget (Piaget & Inhelder, 1969), a child's development of speech has significant ramifications for the development of mental capabilities. Importantly, at this stage a child has the ability to modify behavior within a social context through verbal communications with others. Within this context, the child begins to internalize words and evolve thought processes. And with language, the child can begin to experiment with thought-pictures and is no longer confined to motor responses based on various stimuli.

The underlying mode of thought during stage 2 is intuitive. During this period children are experimenters, explorers, and imitators. They are unconcerned about the exactness of their pronouncements. Their use of sounds and language is often inventive and idiosyncratic. To stimulate this disposition toward language, children need an environment rich in the use of interesting and colorful verbal forms. One aspect of speech during this period is that it is self-centered; children seem to be talking at rather than with others. As in the previous stage where restricting visual stimulation has long-term detrimental effects, denying children the use of their language faculty may result in developmental delays that may be very difficult to correct.

Piaget (Piaget & Inhelder, 1969) has observed that preoperational children's use of intuitive thinking often causes them to misinterpret reality. A child at this stage is generally unable to determine which container holds more water—a tall, narrow beaker or a short, wide one. Often, children's response to this problem is that the taller container holds more water simply because, intuitively, it appears to do so. In educational terms, according to Piaget, it would be unproductive to explain to children at this stage why each container holds the same amount. These children's cognitive structures are simply unable to accommodate this information. Piaget also indicates that stage-2 children have difficulties with reversible relationships. For example, Beth may understand that David is her brother, but she may not understand that she is David's sister. Yet the intuitive approach is a powerful mode of thinking regardless of its apparent illogic. The dynamic and creative nature of intuitive thought provides a means of rapidly learning language and solving problems in new and imaginative ways.

Period of Concrete Operations

The third stage of Piaget's (Piaget & Inhelder, 1969) theory of child development is known as the *period of concrete operations*. Again, children experience an intellectual revolution. Progressing from the free-form thinking of the preoperational stage, they now logically examine the operative relationships among events, objects, and people. Piaget says of operations during this period,

> The operations, such as the union of two classes or the addition of two numbers, are actions characterized by their very great generality since the acts of uniting, arranging in order, etc., enter into all coordinations of particular actions. They are also reversible (the opposite of uniting is separating, the opposite of adding is subtracting, etc.). (Piaget & Inhelder, 1969, pp. 96–97)

These operations occur in conjunction with related systems into which they can be subsumed (e.g., categories, letter and number sequences). And again, the processes are not unique to any individual but rather reflect the functioning of all members of the group at this level of operations.

Unlike children in the intuitive state, stage-2 children are not restricted to understanding through perception. Children in concrete opera-

Young children need concrete experiences with real objects.

tions can decenter their perceptions and understand concrete transformations that events or objects undergo. They can now reverse operations.
Communications also become less egocentric; children begin to talk with
rather than at others. Language becomes functional and purposeful, reflecting children's basic social nature. Piaget (Piaget & Inhelder, 1969) also
found that the concrete operations transformation involves the development of the cognitive structures of seriation and classification. With this
improvement over preoperational thought, children's concepts of space,
time, speed, and causality improve dramatically.

The development of logical operations and the associated capabilities
of reversibility and classification permit children to solve problems more
effectively and surely than during the previous period. But the logic
requires real and observable objects with which to work. Verbal or hypothetical objects or events will not suffice. Thus, within the stage-3 realm,
children are very literal minded; they interpret situations concretely, failing
to understand abstractions. In fact, children subjected to an abstract idea
will convert the abstraction into a specific concrete event relevant to their
experiences. Children will have a difficult time solving a problem presented
in abstract verbal terms. The same children will have far fewer difficulties
when applying the logic of concrete operations to the same problem presented in the form of real and observable objects.

During this period, children express a strong tendency to organize and
apply strict rules to activities they undertake. Concrete operational children

are often more concerned with establishing rules for an activity than with the activity itself. Working out the functional relationship among various elements in an activity is a focal point during the third stage of development. Once children establish relationships and rules for action, they have a particularly difficult time modifying their ideas during this period. They see things distinctly; things are or they are not; subtleties or shades of gray are not acceptable. Altering the rules of a game is a difficult undertaking for children in this stage of intellectual development.

Unless children who are operating concretely are offered direct experiences, preferably hands-on, their learning will be inefficient. To substantiate cognitive growth during this time, practical skills should be taught. When activities such as organizing, constructing, classifying, sorting, counting, and arranging are provided, cognitive development will be engendered.

Period of Formal Operations

According to Piaget (Piaget & Inhelder, 1969), the period called *formal operations* is the fourth and final stage of intellectual development. During this period, the adolescent's cognitive structures mature to the adult level. Piaget's theory predicts that no additional structural improvements will occur beyond the period of formal operations. The efficiency and reach of those structures can be expected to improve during the course of adulthood.

> The great novelty of this stage is that by means of a differentiation of form and content the subject becomes capable of reasoning correctly about propositions he does not believe, or at least not yet; that is propositions that he considers pure hypotheses. (Piaget & Inhelder, 1969, p. 132)

Accordingly, a person operating at this intellectual stage develops the ability to construct plausible conclusions, which provide the basis of formal thought.

The ability to perform logical operations, which began during the concrete operational period, is brought to its full development during stage 4. This final period of cognitive development, however, permits an adolescent a considerably broader range of application of logical operations to problem solving then did the previous period. During the period of concrete operations, children are limited to applying logic to the solution of tangible problems as they occur; they cannot project into the future or consider hypothetical situations. Children who have achieved formal operations, however, possess the capacity to engage all categories and classes of problems. The verbal abstraction, the hypothetical, and consideration of past and future conditions are all subject to the power of the logic of formal operations.

The adolescent operating in formal operations can employ several strategies simultaneously in solving problems. In stage 3, this was not possible; the application of broad and inclusive theories to the solution of a complex, multilayered problem was not conceivable. Within the realm of formal operations, an adolescent can undertake such an effort. Understanding the concept of causation, using scientific reasoning to approach a problem, and building and testing hypotheses are all hallmarks of the fourth stage of Piaget's theory. In addition, adolescents will be able to consider problems involving a combination of several variables rather than centering on one aspect of a problem as they did during the concrete period. They will also be able to undertake complex verbal problems. Problems involving proportion and conservation of movement can also be penetrated by their advanced logic.

For the first time children can separate personal perception from objective reality. The result is the ability to evaluate a logical argument separate from its content. Children in concrete operations are restricted to dealing with the world according to personal perception; thus, they are unable to consider a problem involving blue snow, for example. The more advanced children, however, can deal with such a hypothetical condition and, in fact, derive a logical and valid argument not dependent on the observable reality of white snow. As in the previous stages of development, formal operations evolve directly as a result of the cognitive structures developed during preceding stages. In fact, the cognitive structures formed during the previous periods culminate in those of the final stage. With the transformations that occur from one stage to another, cognitive structures are continuously subject to structural alteration. The assimilation, accommodation, and equilibration processes are constantly at work from the sensorimotor period through the period of formal operations.

Implications for RCM Teachers

From the perspective of cognitive theory, children's development is marked by periods when they are particularly sensitive and responsive to outside influences. However, children are not blank slates on which teachers compose whatever it is they desire. Rather, children—dynamic and ever-changing, composed of inherent dispositions and tendencies, and subject to the external environment—develop and grow in skill and knowledge in an invariable sequence from birth through adolescence and beyond. To assist children through their tumultuous growth, teachers must respond with precision and understanding. To teach effectively, teachers should be aware of the materials and approaches most appropriate for children's readiness to learn. Cognitive theory provides insights and guidance into these issues.

Piaget (Piaget & Inhelder, 1969) has suggested that children's cognitive structures should be carefully considered when presenting instructional materials. According to Piaget's view, intellectual capabilities are not set at birth but, rather, ultimately depend on the appropriateness of the activities and the environment in which children are involved during each of the four periods of growth. RCM teachers should prepare a subject for study in a form and manner that is compatible with children's operating cognitive structures. To do otherwise will diminish the effectiveness of the classroom experience for developing children. To increase the effectiveness of the discipline program, teachers must ensure that children participate in activities that stimulate cognitive development. It is the suitability of the experience that produces cognitive growth and successful children.

A strong presumption in this culture is that an acceleration of intellectual growth is an inherently positive step that should be pursued by educators. An alternative to this position is one that strengthens children's intellectual accomplishments in each period of development. This will serve to improve intellectual capacity and broaden the foundation for future growth. Expanding relevant learning opportunities will improve learning conditions in the classroom by minimizing conditions that serve only to frustrate children's pursuit of knowledge. In classrooms where teachers understand children's intellectual characteristics and knowledge is efficiently presented, effective management can be attained.

PERSONALITY DEVELOPMENT

The development of personality coincides with the development of both the physical and cognitive realms. Discussing the personal–psychological character of development lends greater depth to our understanding of the total child. The development of personality follows a sequence of interdependent periods that generally correspond to the stages of cognitive development (see Table 2–2). The successful satisfaction of needs during one stage determines children's ability to progress to the next stage. When needs are not met, children will have difficulty making the transition to the following stage and, in fact, may be delayed or even prevented from continuing their personal advance to more mature stages of development.

Just as Jean Piaget's theories describe the area of cognitive development, Erik Erikson's (1980) ideas have become the basis for much of our understanding of personality development in children and adolescents.

Erikson's (1980) notions of human development arose out of his work in Freudian psychology. Sigmund Freud, originator of the concepts id, ego, and superego, believed that to understand adult personality and behavior, the experiences and relationships the adult had as a child must be analyzed. Within these experiences and relationships, Freud saw the basis for later emotional development. As he investigated child and adult behavior, he recognized that children and adults move through a series of emotional stages from birth to adulthood. Freud described five such stages: the oral stage, from birth to eighteen months; the anal stage, from eighteen months to three years; the phallic stage, from three to seven years; the period of latency, from seven to twelve years; and the genital period, from twelve years through adulthood. Table 2–3 compares Freud's and Erikson's views.

TABLE 2–2
Cognitive and Personality Stages of Development

Piaget's Cognitive Stages	Approximate Age (range)	Erikson's Personality Stages
Formal operations	18 17 16 15 14 13	Identity vs. diffusion
Concrete operations	12 11 10 9 8	Industry vs. inferiority
Preoperational	7 6 5 4	Initiative vs. guilt
	3 2	Autonomy vs. shame
Sensorimotor	1.5 0	Trust vs. mistrust

Freud found that as children undergo this sequence of emotional transformation, their experiences have a profound effect on the formation of adult personality. These transformative periods are defined by specific areas of personality that are particularly vulnerable to alteration. Based on these periods of change, Erikson (1980) developed eight stages that further define the contents and mechanisms operating in the maturing human being. In the following discussion, we examine the first five stages, which entail the years from birth through adolescence (see Table 2–4).

The first of Erikson's (1980) stages concerns the development of trust and mistrust. Erikson has defined trust as "what is commonly implied in reasonable trustfulness as far as others are concerned." He defines mistrust as characterizing "individuals who withdraw into themselves in particular ways when they are at odds with themselves or with others" (1980, pp. 57–58). The stage of trust versus mistrust occurs during the infant stage, from birth to eighteen months. Erikson has determined that during this time children develop varying degrees of trust and mistrust. To successfully establish a solid foundation on which to build a balanced personality, he believes that parents must provide a highly supportive and nurturing environment. The quality of and degree to which parents attend to children

TABLE 2–3
Comparison of Freud and Erikson: Ages and Stages

Approximate Ages	Freud	Erikson
12–18 years	Genital	Identity–identity diffusion
7–12 years	Latency	Industry–inferiority
3–7 years	Phallic	Initiative–guilt
18 months to 3 years	Anal	Autonomy–shame
Birth to 18 months	Oral	Trust–mistrust

during this period will have a profound effect on the degree to which the maturing children express trust and dependability. When parents provide consistent care and affection during interactive periods, children will be prepared to engage the next level of personal development successfully.

During the second stage of Erikson's (1980) theory, which he designated the period of autonomy versus shame and doubt, children continue their emotional development. Between the ages of eighteen months and three years, children experience the conflict generated by their attempts to gain a degree of competence and independence from their parents. The significance of this period, according to Erikson (1980), depends on the increasing development of the muscles and children's improved ability to harmonize contending actions, such as grasping and releasing, within the domain of increasing will and independence.

While pursuing independence, children begin to express a strong sense of self and engage in a period of intense investigation of their environment. At this stage, children can be easily frustrated by interfering adults who prevent them from fully developing personal autonomy. Therefore, adults at this stage should support children's attempts to explore the world. Also at this time, children begin to express themselves verbally. As noted in the discussion on cognitive development, vocabulary increases several-fold during this period; much practice is required to accomplish this expansion. To increase the probability of success during this stage of development, adults should encourage children to express themselves verbally.

TABLE 2–4
Erikson's Stages of Personality Development

Stage of Development	Approximate Age	Characteristics
V. Identity vs. identity diffusion	12–18 years	Able to use logic to solve hypothetical problems; undergo significant body system alterations, resulting in reproductive capability; make decisions on objective evidence; ideas of others are considered less egocentrically; capable of empathy; develop the need to improve things; require responsibility for growth
IV. Industry vs. inferiority	6–12 years	Focus turns to friends and school; form social alliances reflecting growing interest in other people and in things outside family; need to actively explore the world, to test themselves, and to work hard to achieve goals
III. Initiative vs. guilt	3–6 years	Children begin to explore sexual identity; begin to identify with appropriate male and female models; important to reinforce their identity at this point, to establish a sense of self
II. Autonomy vs. shame	18 months to 3 years	Conflicted by their attempts to gain a degree of independence and competence; begin to express a strong sense of self; intensely investigate environment; should be encouraged to express themselves verbally
I. Trust vs. mistrust	Birth to 18 months	Develop varying degrees of trust and mistrust; parents must provide supportive and nurturing environment; quality of care will have a profound effect on the degree to which the maturing child expresses trust and dependability

Constantly correcting word pronunciations and grammatical forms will often hinder verbal development. Rather than inhibiting children at this time by overcorrection, Erikson (1980) suggests that adults model the speech desired. Accordingly, adults should avoid speaking in unnatural ways, such as baby talk, which will only confuse children's efforts.

There is a clear relationship between parents' behavior during this period and a child's self-confidence and sense of autonomy. The most productive pattern parents can provide is an imaginative environment that stimulates speech and exploration. Supportive parents constantly involve their children in stimulating activities during which they question and elicit children's ideas. This indirect form of teaching, in combination with the experience of self-initiative, establishes the basis for feelings of competence. As children learn independence and begin to see themselves as active and effective participants in the management of their environment, they establish a strong foundation on which to build a healthy and maturing personality.

Yet, children will not always successfully navigate through the demands of this period. Sometimes children develop a sense of shame because of their failure to develop independence effectively. When parents or other adults fail to provide stimulating experiences, restrict activity too narrowly, ignore the need for attention and love, and deny or harshly criticize expression, children will not advance and may be prevented from developing a productive and well-balanced personality. Their sense of shame will limit their ability to engage life directly and confidently.

The third stage of Erikson's (1980) theory concerns initiative and guilt. Children develop these personal characteristics during the third through sixth years. This period especially affects a child's gender identity. Whereas in the previous stage of development, children generally began to explore sexual identity, they now begin to identify with appropriate male and female models and behave in accordance with what they see. It is especially important to reinforce their sexual identity at this point, so they will establish the sense of self needed to successfully advance to the next stage of development.

Children naturally possess feelings of inferiority at this time. To avoid establishing a sense of guilt about their desires and inabilities, they should be assured that they will eventually be able to do what they see adults doing. Taking personal initiative is inherently connected to children's personal identity and overcoming this sense of inferiority. According to Erikson (1980), children possess the capacity to overcome the difficulties of this stage by increasing their areas of confidence and mobility in fulfilling needs and by creatively using imagination and language to explore the world.

When children have been successfully weaned of their sole reliance on adults for meeting their needs, adults will have been successful in supporting them in the development of their personal identity. As children express independence by effectively meeting the demands of various situations, they will develop greater confidence in their own competence and enhance their growing sense of self.

During Erikson's (1980) fourth stage, industry and inferiority are the primary issues. From approximately six until twelve years of age, children turn away from their focus on parents to a more generalized focus on their world, most notably friends and school. During this period, children learn to communicate through others in an increasingly less ego-centered approach. By behaving in this manner, children free themselves from the isolation and control that are related to their total dependence on parents. They become more socially oriented, forming social alliances that reflect their growing interest in other people and in things outside their family and home. During this time, they exert enormous amounts of energy trying to perfect their skills in dealing with the demands of the world. Erikson describes the focus of this period:

> ... while all children need their hours and days of make-believe in games, they all, sooner or later, become dissatisfied and disgruntled without a sense of being useful, without a sense of being able to make things and make them well and even perfectly: this is what I call a sense of industry. Without this, the best-entertained child soon acts exploited. It is as if he knows and his society knows that now that he is psychologically a parent, he must begin to be somewhat of a worker and potential provider before becoming a biological parent. . . . As he once untiringly strove to walk well and to throw things away well, he now wants to make things well. He develops the pleasure of work completion by steady attention and preserving diligence. (1980, p. 91)

Children during middle elementary years enjoy playing and learning with peers of the same gender.

During this period of developing greater self-sufficiency and independence, children are particularly stable emotionally. Also at this period, children experience the concrete operational period, when they see the world as stable and predictable; shades of gray are unwelcome intrusions into their ideas about the world. As children learn new social, practical, and academic skills, they enhance their sense of industry. Where they fail to do so, they develop a sense of inferiority, which further limits their ability to develop personal competence. At this time, it is important to encourage children to actively engage the world, to explore and test themselves, and to work hard to achieve goals. With success comes the knowledge that their efforts have results. Children who fail to develop a sense of industry based on their skill in achieving goals will not achieve independence. Their sense of inferiority will diminish their capacity to meet the demands of the world.

Development of industry during this period occurs to a large extent where children spend most of their active time, in school and among friends. The experience in school is particularly important to children's development of self-confidence and skill mastery. Within the classroom, children can be given the opportunity to learn many new skills, which will result in a growing ability to solve problems competently. With this accomplishment, the promise of adulthood made in an earlier age comes closer to reality.

The final period of personal development relevant to this topic occurs between the ages of twelve and eighteen years. According to Erikson (1980), the formation of identity, or the failure of that formation, which he calls *identity diffusion*, is the main issue of the adolescent age. During this period, children undergo their most tumultuous changes, often causing them to behave in aggressive, confused, and unpredictable ways. It is a time of significant body system alterations that result in physically mature individuals capable of reproduction. But it is also a time when they begin to see the contradictions of the world more clearly, further exacerbating their emotional instability.

> But in puberty and adolescence all sameness and continuities relied on earlier are questioned again because of a rapidity of body growth which equals that of early childhood and because of the entirely new addition of physical genital maturity. The growing and developing young people, faced with the psychological revolution within them, are now primarily concerned with attempts at consolidating their social roles. . . . In their search for a new sense of continuity and sameness, some adolescents have to refight many of the crises of earlier years, and they are never ready to install lasting idols and ideals as guardians of a final identity. (Erikson, 1980, p. 94)

Cognitively, adolescents leave the world of predictability where right and wrong are certain and where their skills have an immediate and direct effect on the environment in which they operate. As adolescents, they begin to evaluate conditions, comparing what they see to what might be. They begin to separate the world around them from their own desires and perceptions. Objective reality begins to assert itself in the adolescent mind. They begin to understand and use metaphorical descriptions. The ideas and positions of others are considered less egocentrically by advancing adolescents. They sometimes can put themselves in another's position, developing empathy and a need to change things.

Alternatively, with greater uncertainty and a heightened sense of self, children become particularly self-conscious as they advance into adolescence. In this state, they try to fit in by conforming to the dictates of peer groups. They can be excessively egotistic, demand attention, and look for as many ways to conform as possible. Their world becomes relativistic, where behavior is tested against their own and others of their group's subjective rationalizations. Conformance to authorities' wishes that they previously accepted is now uncertain.

The effect of this change and uncertainty leads to an adolescent identity crisis. The successful evolution of personality during this period depends on the ability to meet the demands of this stage of personal development successfully. If adolescents overcome the difficulties associated with this period, then it is likely that they will have established a strong foundation for advancement into adulthood. If, on the other hand, they succumb to these conflicts, their personality will not solidify. Instead, it will remain uncertain, diffuse, and alienated with little sense of purpose or satisfaction. To avoid this failure, Erikson (1980) strongly suggests that adolescents be given every opportunity to develop a sense of responsibility for themselves and others. Real, self-directed experience, working to meet the needs of others, and satisfying the demands of society will help adolescents to develop purpose and a strong identity on which to build a mature adulthood.

Implications for RCM Teachers

The scope of Erikson's theory permits us to see the needs and potential problems experienced by all children in their development toward adulthood. Each stage of development requires that adults provide the necessary environment and tools for children to succeed in overcoming the obstacles of the period in which they are operating. Children's behaviors and abilities expressed at each stage of development depend on the degree to which they successfully managed the issues of the preceding stage. If children fail to overcome difficulties or to learn the skills necessary to fulfill their growing responsibilities at any stage, problems will be compounded in each successive stage. Teachers, therefore, should make certain that their instructional effort is effective and that their knowledge of and sensitivity to the transformations of childhood are substantial.

When considering Erikson's ideas about personality development in conjunction with Piaget's theories about intellectual transformation, RCM teachers have at their disposal a powerful perspective from which to view the conditions of childhood and adolescence. Teachers should evaluate their students from this theoretical perspective to determine children's readiness to learn. Teachers will succeed in the classroom when they apply these ideas effectively. Dealing with the intellectual capacity of children as if it exists in isolation, separate from personality, will not lead to effective instruction. This means that RCM teachers must consider the entire child, the cognitive and affective domains, to implement a discipline program that inherently relies on the quality of the underlying instructional program.

MORAL DEVELOPMENT

Similar in structure to the cognitive and personality developmental theories of Piaget and Erikson, Lawrence Kohlberg's (1969) theory of moral development adds another perspective to our understanding of the human condition. The issue of moral development is intrinsically related to both cognitive and personal development. From the earliest interactions with others to a time when older adults no longer can function effectively as thinking individuals, the issue of moral reasoning and behavior is relevant. The capacity to reason, to understand and solve complex problems, and to communicate and empathize with others depends on the degree to which the individual has progressed through the stages of cognitive, personal, and moral development. The importance of understanding the relationship of child development to successful teaching is underscored by John Dewey.

> The aim of education is growth, both intellectual and moral. Only ethical and psychological principles can elevate the school to a vital institution in the greatest of all constructions—the building of a free and powerful character. Only knowledge of the order and connection of the stages in psychological development can insure the maturing of the psychical powers. Education is the work of supplying the conditions which will enable the psychological functions to mature in the freest and fullest manner. (1895/1964, p. 273)

Children experience extraordinary growth and development in the cognitive and personal realms from birth through adolescence. Changes in the capacity for moral reasoning follow along a similar path, though not as certainly or as rapidly. Piaget (1965) explored the moral development of children and observed significant changes in their reasoning. He determined that the onset of moral reasoning does not occur until the age of six. Piaget designated two stages of moral development: the heteronomous and the autonomous. During the heteronomous stage, children view rules as unalterable and absolute. Children at this stage of reasoning believe that breaking a rule automatically leads to reprimand or worse. Children in the second stage of development, however, understand that rules and regulations are made by adults and are often altered according to need. Recogni-

Upper elementary and middle grade students enjoy challenges of real-life problems.

tion of the relative nature of moral thinking gives children greater freedom to explore their relationship to authority. Kohlberg's (1969) theory of moral development, though in agreement with Piaget's basic developmental structure, establishes greater stage specificity and more precise definitions of moral reasoning.

Corresponding to Piaget's discoveries in intellectual and moral development and Erikson's findings in personality development, Kohlberg (1969) determined that moral reasoning develops in an invariable sequence of increasingly more complex stages from birth through adulthood. After long observation and analysis of the reasoning used by individuals to solve various moral dilemmas, Kohlberg concluded that people evolve through six stages of moral development (see Table 2–5). Kohlberg found that these stages are applicable across cultures and classes and from person to person. Within his scheme of development, children cannot achieve a higher stage of moral reasoning without experiencing the preceding stage. This condition clearly reflects Piaget's model of cognitive growth.

To reinforce understanding of Kohlberg's (1969) theory of moral development, we introduce the following situation involving moral decision making in which Kohlberg's stages are exemplified. First, we present the dilemma and then alternative arguments representing each of the six stages after each stage's description.

A poor family consisting of a mother and three children was in ill health. They had inadequate housing and medical care and were

TABLE 2–5
Kohlberg's Categories and Stages of Moral Development

Kohlberg's Categories and Stages of Moral Development	Characteristics
Postconventional	
Stage 6. The universal ethical principle orientation.	Reasoning at the highest level of moral consciousness; ethical principles that guide the solution of moral dilemmas must be logically consistent and broadly applicable; principles are abstract and not dependent on written formulas, such as legal or moral codes of behavior.
Stage 5. The social contract-legalistic orientation	Based on the implicit social contract, which exists between the individual and society; moral dilemmas at this level necessitate an ability to reason abstractly and to consider various arguments and consequences in relation to underlying principles.
Conventional	
Stage 4. The "law and order" orientation	Solution of moral problems by legal authority; laws and legal sanctions are the basis for legitimate action; underlying ethic is to act within legal guidelines to protect the group.
Stage 3. The interpersonal concordance or "good boy–nice girl" orientation	Concerned with pleasing others and receiving their approval; will conform to what the dominant group defines as acceptable thought and action; the intended consequences of an action are judged as important; think in terms of distinct stereotypes; clear idea of right and wrong.
Preconventional	
Stage 2. The instrumental-relativist orientation	Based on satisfying personal needs and desires; acting to meet those desires, determine the rightness or wrongness of the act; aware of the needs of others—will actually work to satisfy those needs when it is to their personal advantage to do so.
Stage 1. The punishment and obedience orientation	Based on the physical exercise of power; those who possess power should be obeyed to avoid punishment; measure rightness or wrongness of an action purely by the physical consequences of the behavior.

undernourished. The father was dead, and the mother was unemployed after losing her unskilled job as the result of a factory closing. The mother became desperate after her request for support from the state was denied. The authorities stated that she had to work if she wanted support. She said she would, but that she could not leave her children sick and unattended. In her desperation, she decided to steal a purse at the local supermarket. She succeeded and found $200 in the purse. She was undecided about repeating the act now that she knew how to help her family.

Kohlberg (1969) offers three major categories in which to place the six stages of moral reasoning. Kohlberg has designated the most basic form of moral reasoning as preconventional. Preconventional moral reasoning is concerned with physical punishment and reward. Children at this level recognize rules as either good or bad, but they consider only the physical or personal consequences as delimiters of their behavior. Within this first category, Kohlberg has indicated two stages: stage 1, the punishment and obedience orientation; and stage 2, the instrumental–relativist orientation.

In stage 1, moral orientation is based on the physical exercise of power. Those who possess power should be obeyed and mollified whenever necessary to avoid punishment. Individuals in stage 1 measure the rightness or wrongness of an action purely by the physical consequences of the behavior. Children can be expected to unquestioningly obey authority at this stage of development, but for no reason other than that the authority has the strength to inflict punishment or bestow rewards. Following is the stage-1 argument in relation to the previously described mother's behavior:

Pro—She should steal the purse to help her family. It's not wrong to take the purse from someone who is so careless. And anyway she has a right to keep her children safe.

Con—Stealing a purse is clearly against established authority and a crime punishable under the law.

A person's behavior at the instrumental level of moral development, stage 2, is based on satisfying personal needs and desires. Acting to meet those desires determines the rightness or wrongness of the act. If the act fails to satisfy the desire, then the act must be wrong. The alternative is true as well for the person operating at the second level of development. Kohlberg (1969) indicates that people at this stage are aware of the needs of others and will actually work to satisfy those needs when it is to their personal advantage to do so. Ideas of fairness, reciprocity, and gratitude are merely conveniences, instruments to personal gain, not the ethical basis for behavior. The stage-2 argument follows:

Pro—It's acceptable to steal because her children's well-being is at stake. She reasons that by stealing she will be able to get the money she needs quickly and return to her children.

Con—To steal the purse is wrong because she could get caught and be put in jail; her children would then be left without a caretaker.

The second category in Kohlberg's (1969) theory is the conventional level of moral reasoning. At this level, the entirely self-centered, self-serving behavior of the first stage gives way to consideration of others. People and social groups, such as the family or nation, are regarded as important in their own right. At this level, conformity and loyalty to established patterns of thinking are expressed.

Within this category, Kohlberg (1969) has defined two stages: stage 3, the interpersonal concordance or "good boy–nice girl" orientation; and stage 4, the "law and order" orientation. In the third stage of development, children are often concerned with pleasing others and receiving their approval. To accomplish this, children will conform to what the dominant group defines as acceptable thought and action. As individuals move further away from the instrumental egotism of the preceding stages, they judge the intended consequences of an action as important. At this level of development, however, people think in terms of distinct stereotypes and clear assessments of right and wrong. Relativism is not yet part of moral reasoning. The stage-3 argument concerning the mother's behavior follows:

Pro—She should steal the purse. She was only doing what a good mother would do in similar circumstances. What blame could be attributed to her acting out of love for her family? If she let her family suffer, she would be blamed for not loving her children adequately.

Con—She shouldn't steal the purse. If her children suffer, she can't be blamed because she was following the law. She is not without feeling. She should find a job and follow the directions of authorities. The authorities are the ones responsible for her children's suffering.

A person involved in stage-4 thinking is guided in the solution of moral problems by legal authority. Laws and legal sanctions are the basis for legitimate action. The individual entering stage 4 continues to move away from egocentric thinking. The underlying ethic here is to act within legal guidelines to protect the group, maintain social harmony, and "do one's duty." Accordingly, established rules and mores reflect tested ideas that must be given sway over free, unfettered expression, which may result in rapid changes and social upheaval. The stage-4 argument follows:

Pro—The mother should steal the purse. If she does nothing, the children will continue to suffer. The mother is responsible for her children's suffering if she does nothing to prevent it. She must steal the purse and continue to steal until her children are well and safe.

Con—Nothing could be more naturally ordained than a mother trying to save her children, but it is wrong to steal. She knows that stealing is wrong and harmful to the person from whom she stole the purse.

Kohlberg's (1969) third category of moral development is the postconventional, autonomous, or principled level. It contains two stages: stage 5, the social contract–legalistic orientation, and stage 6, the universal ethical principle orientation. People operating at this level are concerned with underlying values and principles. Personal moral reasoning is independent of declarations issued by legal or moral authorities. Operating at these stages requires sophisticated reasoning and problem-solving abilities.

Stage-5 reasoning is based on the implicit social contract that exists between the individual and society. The rights of the individual are predicated on that agreement. To the postconventional thinker, underlying principles determine the acceptability of particular laws. Being able to solve moral dilemmas at this level necessitates an ability to reason abstractly and to consider various arguments and consequences in relation to underlying principles. Even after establishing a position, stage-5 reasoners can adjust their ideas once additional evidence has been considered. Importantly, the supporting principles at this level of moral reasoning must be universally applicable. A stage-5 argument in relation to the mother's behavior follows:

> Pro—The mother must save her children. Left with no other options that will not result in harm to someone, she decides to steal from a person who appears to be well off and will be hurt very little by the loss of the purse. She knows that stealing the purse is wrong, but she is justified.

> Con—Stealing in these circumstances is understandable but doesn't justify the harm that may result from her action. Even if you accept the notion that the victim may not suffer very much, the mother has no right to inflict suffering on an innocent victim.

At stage 6, a person is reasoning at the highest level of moral consciousness. Concern here is that chosen ethical principles that guide the solution of moral dilemmas are logically consistent and broadly applicable. Principles at this stage of development are abstract and independent of written formulas, such as legal or moral codes of behavior. Kohlberg says, "At heart, these are universal principles of justice, of the reciprocity and equality of the human rights and of the respect for the dignity of human beings as individual persons" (1973, p. 8). A stage-6 argument follows:

> Pro—This situation forces the mother to choose between saving her children and stealing. The moral imperative requires her to care for her children and accept the consequences of her act.

> Con—This situation forces the mother to choose between her children's well-being and the well-being of another. Her decision to steal should not be made in relation to her children only, but in relation to all those who will be affected by her action, while considering the right of everyone to live free of suffering.

Students during the adolescent years are able to address complex verbal problems.

Implications for RCM Teachers

The relationship of Kohlberg's ideas concerning the invariable, sequential nature of moral development to Piaget's theory is evident; however, the ages at which stage-change occurs and the time required to make these transformations do not necessarily correspond. Some delay may occur between the onset of a particular level of cognitive development and the occurrence of a similar level of moral reasoning. The degree of complexity operating in the solution of a moral dilemma may be sufficiently great to constrain a person from applying the cognitive capability developed at a particular stage of intellectual development. Unless children undertake sufficient practice in solving moral dilemmas at or one stage above their actual stage of intellectual and moral development, they will lack the skill and confidence to engage problems effectively at the level at which they are capable of doing so.

At the upper levels of moral reasoning, this may be especially true. Adolescents will be unable to solve moral dilemmas with stage 5 or 6 levels of reasoning unless they have actually achieved formal operations. Until individuals have developed sophisticated reasoning and have had the opportunity to test their ideas, it is unlikely that moral reasoning will actually match cognitive capacity at the upper stages of moral development.

Interestingly, when presented with solutions to moral dilemmas, children tend to select solutions representing one stage greater than their current level of thinking. This situation is likely due to the fact that children can understand ideas one level beyond their current stage of cognitive development. The need to assimilate and accommodate ideas permits children to construct cognitive structures that include more complete and complex solutions to problems. Faced with a more adequate solution to a problem than the one they are currently employing, children will recognize the potential power in the new approach and make an effort to accommodate it. This condition permits teachers to present ideas to children that will stimulate them to learn new and more appropriate solutions to moral dilemmas. By expanding their moral consciousness, students will develop a greater understanding of teacher expectations in the classroom. Children will, however, be limited by their operating level of cognitive development. If teachers understand children's level of moral reasoning, they can work to assist children in overcoming the obstacles to appropriate classroom behavior.

Critically, attainment of higher-level reasoning depends on the degree to which children are given adequate opportunity to experience increasingly greater levels of responsibility. When given responsibility for doing so, children can put into action their understanding of moral issues. This experience will help them gain the self-confidence necessary to behave according to their beliefs in the face of conflict.

As children move into more complex levels of moral reasoning, they become less self-centered. This gives teachers the opportunity to explore the effects of unacceptable behavior on others in the classroom. The use of role playing may give students direct insight into the relationship of behavior to beliefs. Teachers must remember, however, that a correspondence between the complexity of any discussions or activities undertaken to develop moral reasoning and the child's stage of intellectual development must exist. Children's understanding and behavior are often at odds. Achieving correspondence between moral reasoning and behavior takes practice, self-examination, and patience.

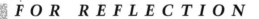

FOR REFLECTION

What basic generalizations can you conclude from this discussion of theories of development?

PUTTING CONCEPTS INTO PRACTICE

Questions for Review and Discussion

1. Identify which of the following statements are incorrect, and then make the necessary corrections.

   a. At school age, children begin to favor one side of the body over the other.

   b. By the time most children reach age three, they will have already learned such skills as buttoning and zipping pants and jackets, buckling belts, cutting with scissors, and coloring within predetermined borders.

   c. After the seventh year, most children continuously improve the quality of their fine and gross motor skills, introducing many entirely new basic capabilities.

   d. From their eighth through tenth birthdays, boys are generally larger than girls.

   e. By their sixth year, children's improved balance, eyesight, and dexterity permit them to engage in complex activities, such as playing musical instruments or constructing complicated models such as cars and aircraft.

   f. By the end of the fourth grade, many boys will have begun to gain height and weight over girls. They will maintain this advantage until the eleventh or twelfth year, when girls begin their major growth period.

   g. With the onset of female menstruation at approximately age fifteen and male ejaculation by age thirteen, girls and boys enter puberty.

   h. Some people may fully mature in as little as thirty-six months from onset, whereas some others may require three or five years.

   i. Early onset of puberty in either sex places little stress on the person experiencing it, whereas late onset is significantly stressful.

2. Which of the following statements best describes Piaget's theory of cognitive development?

   a. The age at which a child enters a stage of cognitive development is precisely established, but the sequence is variable.

   b. The beginning of each stage varies considerably for each child, but boys commence each stage sooner than girls.

   c. Though the sequence of each stage is invariable, the age at which a child begins a stage can vary considerably.

   d. Children can skip stages through effort or natural capability.

3. Which of the following statements concerning the cognitive growth and development processes of accommodation, assimilation, and equilibration are incorrect? Make the necessary corrections.

   a. Assimilation, accommodation, and equilibration are the means by which children integrate new experiences into cognitive structures.

   b. Schemata develop from birth, when they are highly differentiating.

   c. The number of schemata established during the first months of life remains the same through adolescence.

   d. Children who assimilate everything they encounter will develop many schemata.

   e. Children who readily accommodate experiences will develop many schemata.

   f. Cognitive equilibrium is achieved when children learn to use either assimilation or accommodation as their primary means of adjustment.

4. Indicate the stage of cognitive development described by the following statements:

   Sensorimotor   1   Preoperational   2
   Concrete operational   3   Formal operational   4

   a. Unless children operating at this stage are offered direct experiences, preferably hands-on, their learning will be inefficient.

   b. Understanding the concept of causation, using scientific reasoning to approach a problem, and building and testing hypotheses are all hallmarks of this stage of development.

   c. Children move from a period of simple reflexes to a period when representation of unseen objects readily occurs.

   d. For the first time children can logically examine the operative relationships among events, objects, and people.

   e. The verbal abstraction, the hypothetical, and consideration of past and future conditions are all subject to the power of the logic of children operating at this level of cognitive operations.

   f. During this period, children rapidly extend their capacity to store information, such as words and the implicit rules of language. Their application and understanding of vocabulary increase substantially.

   g. During this period, children express a strong tendency to organize and apply strict rules to activities they undertake.

   h. One aspect of speech during this period is that it is self-centered; children seem to be talking at, rather than with, others.

   i. Children of this age group have no basis on which to build categories for organizing reality.

j. Children at this stage can decenter their perceptions and understand observable transformations that events or objects undergo.

k. Children operating at this stage possess the capacity to engage all categories and classes of problems.

l. The logic used by children at this stage requires that they work with real and observable objects. Verbal or hypothetical objects or events will not suffice.

m. Restricting or denying a child strong visual experiences during this period may cause deficits in the development of important cognitive structures.

n. The underlying mode of thought during this stage is intuitive.

o. Piaget found that this cognitive transformation involves the development of the cognitive structures of seriation and classification.

5. Name the Freudian stage of development that corresponds to the Eriksonian stage indicated.

phallic   genital   anal   latency   oral

a. Trust versus mistrust

b. Autonomy versus shame

c. Initiative and guilt

d. Industry and inferiority

e. Identity versus identity diffusion

6. After each of the following descriptive statements, indicate which of the Eriksonian stages it describes.

Trust versus mistrust

Autonomy versus shame

Initiative versus guilt

Industry versus inferiority

Identity versus identity diffusion

a. At this stage Erikson suggests that it is important that children be given real, self-directed experience. Working to meet the needs of others and satisfying the demands of society will help them to develop purpose and a strong identity.

b. Children turn away from their focus on parents to a more generalized focus on the world in which they find themselves, most notably on friends and school.

c. Children at this stage of development can put themselves in another's position, developing empathy and a need to change things.

d. Children now begin to identify with appropriate male and female models.

e. The degree and quality of parental attention to children during this period will have a profound effect on the degree to which maturing children express dependability.

f. Children become more socially oriented, forming various social alliances that reflect their growing interest in other people and in things outside their family and home.

g. It is a time of significant body system alterations that result in physically mature individuals capable of reproduction.

h. Children experience the conflict generated by their attempts to gain a degree of competence and independence from their parents. To increase the probability of success during this stage of development, children should be encouraged to express themselves verbally.

i. At this time, it is particularly important to encourage children to actively engage the world; to explore and test themselves; and to work hard to achieve goals.

7. Indicate the stage of moral development to which each statement refers.

Stage 1: the punishment and obedience orientation

Stage 2: the instrumental–relativist orientation

Stage 3: the interpersonal concordance or "good boy–nice girl" orientation

Stage 4: the "law and order" orientation

Stage 5: the social contract–legalistic orientation

Stage 6: the universal ethical principle orientation

a. The underlying ethic here is to act within legal guidelines to protect the group, maintain social harmony, and "do one's duty."

b. A child at this stage of development will conform to what the dominant group defines as acceptable thought and action.

c. Principles at this stage of development are abstract and not dependent on written formulas, such as legal or moral codes of behavior.

d. People at this stage are aware of the needs of others and will actually work to satisfy those needs when it is to their personal advantage to do so.

e. Those who possess power should be obeyed and mollified whenever necessary to avoid punishment.

f. Ideas of fairness, reciprocity, and gratitude are merely conveniences, instruments to personal gain.

g. Reasoning at this level is based in the implicit social contract that exists between the individual and the overall society.

h. At this level of development, people think in terms of distinct stereotypes and clear assessments of right and wrong.

   i.   The concern here is that chosen ethical principles that guide the solution of moral dilemmas are logically consistent and broadly applicable.

   j.   The rightness or wrongness of an action is measured purely by the physical consequences of the behavior.

   k.   Children are often concerned with pleasing others and receiving their approval.

   l.   The supporting principles at this level of moral reasoning must be universally applicable.

  m. Laws and legal sanctions are the primary basis for legitimate action.

Answer Key

1a. Generally before school begins.

1b. By age five they will have learned these skills.

1c. Few new skills are introduced.

1d. Both sexes are very similar in size.

1e. Skills are not developed by six years; rather, nine years is typical.

1f. Girls are larger during this period.

1g. Girls, age thirteen; boys, age thirteen to sixteen.

1h. Eighteen months up to six years.

1i. Both times are stressful.

2. c.

3b. Simple and undifferentiating.

3c. The number increases dramatically.

3d. Few schemata.

3f. Dominance by either process would result in too many or too few schemata.

4a. 3.

4b. 4.

4c. 1.

4d. 3.

4e. 4.

4f. 2.

4g. 3.

4h. 2.

4i. 1.

4j. 3.

4k. 4.

4l. 3.

4m. 1.

4n. 2.

4o. 3.

5a. Oral.

5b. Anal.

5c. Phallic.

5d. Latency.

5e. Genital.

6a. Identity versus identity diffusion.

6b. Industry versus inferiority.

6c. Identity versus identity diffusion.

6d. Initiative versus guilt.

6e. Trust versus mistrust.

6f. Industry versus inferiority.

6g. Identity versus identity diffusion.

6h. Autonomy versus shame.

6i. Industry versus inferiority.

7a. Stage 4.

7b. Stage 3.

7c. Stage 6.

7d. Stage 2.

7e. Stage 1.

7f. Stage 2.

7g. Stage 5.

7h. Stage 3.

7i. Stage 6.

7j. Stage 1.

7k. Stage 2.

7l. Stage 5.

7m. Stage 4.

REFERENCES

Dewey, J. (1964). In R. D. Archambault (Ed.), *On education: selected writings*. New York: The Modern Library. (Original work published 1895)

Erikson, E. H. (1980). *Identity and the life cycle*. New York: W. W. Norton.

Gesell, A. (1971). *Studies in child development*. Westport, CT: Greenwood Press. (Original work published 1948)

Kohlberg, L. (1969). Stage and sequence: the cognitive developmental approach to socialization. In D. Goslin (Ed.), *Handbook of socialization theory and research*. Chicago: Rand McNally.

Kohlberg, L. (1973). Implications of developmental psychology for education: Examples for moral education. *Educational Psychologist, 10,* 12–14.

Kohlberg, L. (1987). *Child psychology and childhood education*. New York: Longman.

Piaget, J. (1954). *The construction of reality in the child* (M. Cook, Trans.). New York: Basic Books.

Piaget, J. (1965). *The moral judgment of the child* (M. Gabain, Trans.). New York: The Free Press.

Piaget, J., & Inhelder, B. (1969). *The psychology of the child*. New York: Basic Books.

Rohwer, R. D., Ammon, P. R., & Cramer, P. (1974). *Understanding intellectual development*. Hinsdale, IL: Dryden Press.

SUGGESTED READINGS

Bee, H. (1992). *The developing child* (6th ed.). New York: HarperCollins.

Children's Defense Fund. (1989). *A vision for America's future*. Washington, DC: National Association for the Education of Young Children.

Coleman, J. (1990). *Equality and achievement in education*. Boulder, CO: Westview Press.

Goleman, D. (1995). *Emotional intelligence*. New York: Bantam Books.

Gross, F. L. (1987). *Introducing Erik Erikson: An invitation to his thinking*. New York: University Press of America.

Designing the
RCM Environment

A first-year teacher writes to her elementary methods professor:

Dear Dr. Smith:

Is my life supposed to be like this? Yesterday, after teaching school all day, I found myself running out the door as the custodian was locking the building to leave. I was in a major panic as I suddenly realized that I had spent the last hour comparing notes with colleagues to determine who has the worst-behaved kids and, as a result, had left with today's lesson plans incomplete. As I carried twenty boxes of instructional materials to my car, I was mistaken for an employee of a major moving-van line. Once I arrived at home, I prepared a seven-course dinner, cleaned the house, and got the children to bed before sitting down to reflect upon the day's events. I wondered why I had to tell Marvin three times to put the crayons in the box. I felt guilty for losing my temper with three girls who continued to play after I gave clear directions for them to complete center work. I was close to a nervous breakdown as I wondered what miracle I must perform to get Jason to turn in his homework. I had a choice either to crash on the bed in total exhaustion, complete tomorrow's lesson plans, or read the want ads for a new career in the morning's paper, which, by the way, was still rolled. I crashed on the sofa before I could make the choice. Is this what teaching is all about?

Sincerely,

Jane D.

CORRELATES FOR TEACHING RESPONSIBILITY

Relax, there is hope for Jane. Responsible Classroom Management (RCM) for teachers and students is an exciting and creative approach for teaching responsibility to students while effectively teaching children to manage their own behavior. RCM is based on evidence we collected in schools using the RCM plan. We found the following correlates in teaching responsibility:

1. Approximately 88% of students do not require disciplinary action by the teacher.
2. Teachers who are responsible educators can promote and assist students to be responsible.
3. Responsibility can be learned by any student, regardless of family or socioeconomic limitations.
4. Students can achieve higher levels of responsibility when teachers provide clear instructional objectives, use interactive methods of instruction, and have high expectations for appropriate behavior.
5. Students can learn to resolve conflicts and solve their own problems in a responsible manner.

Students can learn to resolve conflicts and solve their own problems in a responsible manner.

One of the basic premises of RCM is that students can learn responsibility. To succeed with this approach, it is important for teachers to be effective instructors. Furthermore, it is imperative that teachers be responsible adults. Irresponsible adults are ineffective in assisting students in becoming responsible because they cannot appropriately model responsible behavior or make the best decisions in providing guidance for children or youth.

NEED FOR THE PROGRAM

Reform efforts will have limited effects on the academic achievement of students until educators, parents, and communities repair school discipline.

Since the 1950s, there have been several major reform movements in education in the United States. Reactions to the launch of *Sputnik* in 1957, the attack on education presented in the 1983 document *A Nation at Risk* (U.S. Department of Education, 1983), and the development of national goals in the 1990s have brought a plethora of national standards and organized programs to restructure the public schools. With respect to the national goals, America 2000 and Goals 2000 place great emphasis on responsible citizenship. For students to grow into participatory members of society, they must gain personal and social responsibility. In America 2000 and Goals 2000, responsibility is directly mentioned in two of the goals and indirectly implied for teachers, parents, and students in the remaining goals. One goal specifically focuses on discipline.

America 2000

In April 1991 President George Bush and the nation's governors held an educational summit (without any educators) in Charlottesville, Virginia, and produced a document entitled *America 2000: An Education Strategy* (U.S. Department of Education, 1991). Contained in the document were six major goals designed to lead the nation through school restructuring and to regain the United States' status as a leader of nations. The six goals for the year 2000 follow:

1. All children in America will start school ready to learn.
2. The high school graduation rate will increase to at least 90%.
3. American students will leave grades four, eight, and twelve having demonstrated competency in challenging subject matter including English, mathematics, science, history, and geography; and every school in America will ensure that all students learn to use their minds well, so they may be prepared for responsible citizenship, further learning, and productive employment in the nation's modern economy.
4. United States students will be first in the world in science and mathematics achievement.
5. Every adult American will be literate and will possess the knowledge and skills necessary to compete in a global economy and exercise the rights and responsibilities of citizenship.
6. Every school in America will be free of drugs and violence and will offer a disciplined environment conducive to learning.

The intentions of the authors of America 2000 exceeded listing a set of national goals and establishing a time line for reaching these goals. America 2000 was intended to be a strategy for restructuring the public schools.

Reactions to America 2000

In the 1992 Gallup/Phi Delta Kappa Education Poll (Elam, Rose, & Gallup, 1992), the public was asked to indicate its awareness of the six national goals. Of the population sampled, 285 or less of 1306 adults, were aware of the six national goals. The percentages were slightly less when the data were analyzed with respect to respondents with no children in schools.

Thirty-three percent of public school parents were aware of goal 1, "By the year 2000, all children in America will start school ready to learn."

The public school parents also exceeded the general population and the population with no children in school in awareness of all goals, scoring near or slightly above the 30% level except in one area. Of interest, awareness of goal 4, "By the year 2000, American students will be first in the world in mathematics and science achievement," was lowest for public school parents, with 22% of those respondents aware of this goal. Surprisingly, the final group in the study, the nonpublic school parents, indicated greatest awareness of goal 4, with a total score of 32%. This group also scored the highest on the awareness scale of all groups with goal 3, "By the year 2000, American students will leave grades four, eight, and twelve having demonstrated competency in challenging subject matter, including English, mathematics, science, history, and geography," with a total of 36% aware of this goal. In the remaining areas (goals 1, 2, 5, and 6), public school parents scored higher than nonpublic school parents.

In the same Gallup poll, these groups were asked to rate the progress being made toward achieving each goal. An overwhelmingly negative perception of the progress of America 2000 was given by the respondents. In fact, for each goal

> more than twice as many people believe that little or no progress has been made as believe that there has been a great deal or quite a bit of progress. . . . nearly one-fourth for each goal did not answer the question or held no opinion. (Elam et al., 1992, p. 46)

Goals 2000

In 1993, newly elected President Bill Clinton appointed former governor of South Carolina Richard W. Riley as the new Secretary of Education to lead the national reform efforts in education. Secretary Riley lost no time in organizing a legislative package for submission to Congress. Riley had been extremely successful as an education governor in South Carolina, leading his state in improving test scores, increasing teacher salaries, developing business and school partnerships, and achieving a "bottom-up approach" to restructuring schools (Young, 1993). The legislation developed under the leadership of Riley in the Clinton administration expanded the elements of America 2000. Termed by President Clinton as "reinventing education," the new legislation became law on March 31, 1994, and is known as Goals 2000: Educate America Act.

Goals 2000: Educate America Act (U.S. Department of Education, 1994) included the original six goals of America 2000 and two additional goals to achieve by the year 2000:

1. All children in America will start school ready to learn. (School Readiness Goal)
2. The high school graduation rate will increase to at least 90%. (School Completion Goal)

3. All students will leave grades four, eight, and twelve having demonstrated competency over challenging subject matter including English, mathematics, science, foreign languages, civics and governments, economics, the arts, history, and geography, and every school in America will ensure that all students learn to use their minds well, so they may be prepared for responsible citizenship, further learning, and productive employment in the nation's modern economy. (Student Achievement and Citizenship Goal)
4. United States students will be first in the world in mathematics and science achievement. (Mathematics and Science Goal)
5. Every adult American will be literate and will possess the knowledge and skills necessary to compete in a global economy and exercise the rights and responsibilities of citizenship. (Adult Literacy Lifelong Learning Goals)
6. Every school in the United States will be free of drugs, violence, and the unauthorized presence of firearms and alcohol and will offer a disciplined environment conducive to learning. (Safe, Disciplined, and Alcohol-and-Drug-Free School Goal)
7. The nation's teaching force will have access to programs for the continued improvement of the professional skills and the opportunity to acquire the knowledge and skills needed to instruct and prepare all American students for the next century. (Teacher Education and Professional Development Goal)
8. Every school will promote partnerships that will increase parental involvement and participation in promoting the social, emotional, and academic growth of children. (Parental Participation Goal)

There is much discussion on how realistic these goals are and if these will remain. A major focal point of the goals is an emphasis on citizenship, in the sense that the schools will produce responsible individuals who will engage in participatory citizenship. A main element of citizenship is, obviously, acting responsibly. Responsible citizens are involved. They correct mistakes and practice socially acceptable behavior. Responsible students self-correct inappropriate behavior as a result of experiencing natural consequences for their acts. A responsible child is not a discipline problem.

GENERAL DISCIPLINE TECHNIQUES

During the past decade, concern over ineffective and inappropriate student discipline techniques currently in use in the nation's schools has escalated. Discipline approaches vary from school to school, but techniques usually fall under one of three major categories: brute technique, rules technique, and paper child technique.

Brute Technique

The first category contains variations of what we call the *brute technique.* In this approach, teachers or principals use scare tactics in a futile attempt to frighten children to do what is expected. Educators use overbearing physical size, emotional outbursts or threats, and corporal punishment to externally control students by creating fear, shame, or pain. This approach is limited in successfully changing undesirable behavior in children. In modern times, the brute technique is damaging and archaic.

Rules Technique

The second category removes the teacher's professional judgment from the selection of appropriate consequences for classroom behavior management. The rules technique fares somewhat better than the brute technique in controlling inappropriate student behavior; however, it is limited in guiding children to responsible actions because their behavior is externally controlled by teachers. Through this approach to classroom behavior management, teachers are limited in opportunities for flexibility in determining the punishment or consequence. Every student is disciplined in the same way, regardless of how effective that discipline may be for different individuals. For example, suspension for fighting may alarm one student and be welcomed by another. Emphasis is placed on the number of offenses as opposed to the nature of the individual offense. In a comparison to the legal system, this equates two criminals receiving equal punishment for robbery and murder. In a similar comparison, if robbery were committed after a murder, the greater punishment would be for the robbery, because it was the second law or rule broken. In other words, the punishment may not fit the crime.

Paper Child Technique

The third category is the paper child technique. Children are considered to be extremely fragile and never criticized or told "no." The model is based on the belief that children need to learn through a controlled world and never should be allowed to experience any negative situations. Ironically, children are permitted to voice their dislikes and dissatisfaction with their peers and teachers, but are themselves praised exclusively. Allowing children to voice their concerns can be healthy, but the overuse of positive rewards and praise is not realistic preparation for adulthood in American society.

As in the rules technique, educators using the paper child technique use tangible rewards or bribes for successful completion of required activities. Although the use of tangible rewards may be appropriate for kindergarten-age children, rewards soon become the expectation, and the expectation for rewards increases with age. In other words, children develop a "what will you give me?" attitude that is damaging to their educational experience, their perception of social responsibility, and teacher sanity. The real sadness is that children do not develop internal control and instead depend totally on the teacher for direction and control.

Classroom teachers and prospective teachers realize that the irresponsible behaviors practiced by children are seeds for problems ranging from simple attention seeking to outright resistance and violence. Unfortunately, these behavior problems may be a result of parents' and teachers' rescuing children from experiencing self-correcting, logical consequences. If parents and educators do not refocus their attention on responsible student behavior, children will not grow into responsible adults.

Today, many children learn early that *no* at best means *maybe,* and after the third perceived *maybe,* the word *no* has no meaning at all. Once children enter formal schooling, this attitude is frequently tolerated. It then generates a pattern of irresponsible behavior that children view as appropriate. Once this occurs, it is almost impossible to reverse.

Why do parents and teachers permit irresponsible behavior? Possibly, because they are so fearful of damaging children's self-esteem that they feel guilty if they do not allow children to have their way. Adults appear to be more concerned with promoting happiness than providing guidance. Providing guidance allows children to learn through honest mistakes and difficult experiences—exercises that promote responsibility. Children must learn that consequences follow every action. This is true whether the consequence is positive or negative. Parents and teachers must no longer protect children from logical or natural consequences.

Because the previously described techniques or combinations of those techniques have minimal effectiveness, and because the development of healthy self-esteem and responsible behavior are educational goals, we developed the RCM plan.

F O R   R E F L E C T I O N

Can you recall any specific teacher who used one or more of these techniques: the brute, rules, or paper child technique?

PRINCIPLES OF THE RCM PLAN

Educators who have had major success with the RCM plan adhere to the following basic program principles:

1. To have responsible students, teachers must be responsible.
2. Teachers state instructional objectives clearly.
3. Responsibility is taught and incorporated instructionally through-out the year.
4. The classroom environment is warm and inviting.
5. Instruction is interactive, and student classroom participation is high.
6. Standards and guidelines replace rigid school and classroom rules.
7. Children are treated fairly but not always disciplined in the same manner.
8. Consequences are used to teach students to self-correct inappro-priate behaviors and to assume responsibility for their actions.
9. Student performance and responsibility are encouraged and acknowledged. Bribery and predetermined rewards are not used.
10. Students practice internal behavior control rather than having their behavior controlled externally.

RESEARCH FINDINGS FROM THE RCM PILOT SCHOOLS

During the 1993–1994 school year, we conducted a national study to field test the RCM plan. First, we extended invitations to the state departments of public instruction to inform schools in their state of the opportunity to participate in the study.

We received more than three hundred inquiries, and we selected a total of 125 schools in 32 states in the first phase of the study. In the first phase, we sent a two-hour video training program, trainer guide, and workbooks to the principals of the schools to direct implementation of the program.

In the second phase of the study, we sent additional materials, includ-ing ideas for consequences, to the schools along with the first survey. Sev-eral of the schools asked if they could do the program next year, stating time problems for training and other previous obligations. Several schools decided not to participate because of a change in administration or lack of support by the faculty, decreasing the study group to sixty-eight schools. By the end of the study, the sixty-eight schools had fully implemented the pro-gram and had collected the data we requested.

We analyzed the data, confirmed the five correlates previously stated at the beginning of this chapter, and concluded the following results:

- Schools reported an 81% drop in office referrals.
- School suspensions decreased by nearly 70%.
- Intensive Care Units (ICUs, defined in Chapter 4) were effec-tive up to three visits. After the first visit, 78% of students were not sent back to ICU. After the second visit, slightly more than

64% of the students were not sent back for corrective action in the ICU.

- Students sent to the ICU for a third visit were placed on a Behavior Improvement Agreement (BIA, defined in Chapter 4).
- The students placed on BIAs represented slightly less than 3% of the school population.
- When students were placed on teacher BIAs, only about one third were broken and referred to the principal.
- Principals' BIAs were broken at a rate of about 50%. Severe and/or legal consequences were used by principals with students who broke the principals' BIAs.

Urban and Rural Research Schools

The sixty-eight schools were basically balanced between rural and urban settings. Urban schools were in large urban areas such as New York City, Milwaukee, Memphis, Charlotte, Dallas, Portland, and Kansas City. Rural areas ranged from very small communities to larger towns that would still be considered rural as compared to large urban areas.

Findings in the rural and urban areas were similar. Suspension and office referrals were lowered in both areas, approximately a drop of 80%. In the urban schools, the rate of students going to the ICU was slightly higher rate than in the rural schools. Additionally, suspension rates, which lowered significantly, were higher in the urban schools.

In the following years, we established several model schools to further test the RCM Plan. In these schools, the data were similar. With improvements to the models during the year before we wrote this book, schools using the plan showed even greater results. Exemplary models for elementary, middle, and secondary schools are presented in Chapter 5.

An experienced teacher is aware that no two children are identical in performance or behavior. However, continued analysis of the behavior patterns of students reveals interesting conclusions. First, as mentioned, in an average class, approximately 88% of the students needed little disciplinary action. Most of the time, they simply did what was required. Often, it was necessary to restate expectations or give students reminders. These students did not cause the teacher great stress or frustration from a behavioral viewpoint; however, at least half of them lacked responsibility, according to the teachers in the project, and needed additional direction.

Another 9% of students were not major problems, but did require more attention to off-task or inappropriate behaviors. Many of these students were attention seekers or extremely active children who got off-task easily. Of special interest, most of these students were above average in ability.

Now, to the real challenge—the remaining 3%. These students came to school with a plethora of problems. They were more likely to be noncompliant in behavior. They demonstrated aggression, anger, and mistrust in their attitudes and actions toward the teacher and the school. Many times, these students had been abused by primary caregivers or mistreated by former teachers. Many students who were abused or mistreated became conforming or withdrawn; some acted out their anger. Many of these students were not provided experiences leading to the development of healthy emotional responses and interactions. For example, without proper guidance, children may develop mistrust or self-doubt, which might be expressed in the classroom. These children have what we term *developmental impairments*. They are not obedient or responsible. Much of their acting-out behavior can also have a ripple effect on other students in the class, especially the 9% who require more attention or get off-task easily.

Additionally, on a responsibility spectrum (see Figure 3–1), students will vary greatly. Students at the upper end of the spectrum tend to be self-correcting, use an internal locus of control, accept consequences, and follow guidelines to a much greater degree than students at the lower end of the spectrum. The students in the lower 12% cause teachers greater frustration and stress. However, a vast majority of students with developmental impairments can be taught responsibility, at least to some degree. Student obedience is the first goal for teachers; obedience must occur first with these students before student responsibility can be learned. Teaching responsibility to these students will require patience, consistency, and understanding. On the whole, children do not want to misbehave. Often, they feel they have no choice.

Humans go through several stages of development from birth to death. Success in school can be related to appropriate developmental experiences early in life. As young children grow, they must find balance in social interactions with others to become developmentally healthy. Children who have parents who are good models and who have encouraged and guided their children appropriately usually are well-adjusted children when they arrive at school. They are also creative, inquisitive, and have a strong desire to learn. On the other hand, students who come from families with developmental impairments or have parents with needs more important than the needs of their children may exhibit behaviors quite opposite to

FIGURE 3–1
Responsibility Spectrum

those of well-adjusted children or children who are healthy developmentally. It is imperative that educators and caregivers realize that meeting children's basic need to belong is paramount to their success.

SCHOOL AND CLASSROOM MANAGEMENT DESIGN

The RCM plan is a classroom management system that differs from those most widely available today. No longer should the teacher monitor structured, inflexible rules that may not be appropriate or educationally sound. Instead, students will learn to adapt to socially acceptable standards and guidelines. In the RCM plan, being fair to students is more important and effective than treating everyone the same. Student self-monitoring with necessary teacher guidance will lead to responsible students with responsible actions. This plan provides instruction in how to handle discipline problems effectively and successfully.

BEHAVIOR CORRECTION

Many times educators try to make children too obedient. Some parents have behaved similarly. At first glance, obedience is a positive concept. There is probably nothing wrong with desiring children to be obedient. However, if techniques used to secure obedience are improperly used or if obedience is abusively forced on children, they may respond negatively. Do citizens pay taxes because it is the responsible thing to do? Or do citizens pay taxes to avoid prison? Suffice it to say that people do some things out of obedience and other things over which they have more control as a result of their value of responsibility. The same is true for children. Children must respond obediently in some situations, but with greater autonomy, they can make responsible choices. Children are incredibly honest and have a great sense of fairness. Students should be allowed to experience consequences to self-correct their behavior and become more responsible as they internalize appropriate behavior.

STUDENT OWNERSHIP

The school and classroom climate should promote student ownership. Students should feel a sense of belonging by being involved in responsible decision making. Faculty members who have input into schoolwide decisions feel a greater sense of ownership and self-worth than if they are given a directive to be obedient to the principal's directives. Many times students who have difficulty controlling their behavior feel that all they receive are directives and limitations. At times, this may be all these students can handle. Unfortunately, many of their actions occur in response to an external locus of control or are precipitated by a miscued internal reaction such as attention deficit disorder or stabilization of medication. For example, these students may do a task for a specified reward. However, if embarrassed or angered, they may rebel, using inappropriate language that they have internalized from their environment and disrupting classroom instruction. Teachers cannot meet the needs of this type of student when twenty-five others are receiving instruction. Of greater importance, it is not fair to teachers or the other students when a disruptive student interrupts their learning. The RCM plan, as described in Chapter 4, provides directions in handling this student effectively with limited emotional stress.

DEVELOPMENTAL ASPECTS OF BEHAVIOR

As presented in Chapter 2, every adult goes through the developmental stages that students experience. Children from healthy homes and caring environments come to school excited and eager to learn. Their parents or other caregivers provided guidance and appropriate boundaries and assisted their children in every stage of their physical, emotional, and intellectual development. What did these parents do right? There is probably no completely definitive answer. However, these parents probably served as good role models and gave much of their time and attention to their children. Growing up is hard work.

Experienced educators are aware that numerous factors and situational influences affect a student's behavior in the classroom. Some of these follow:

1. Every child moves through various developmental stages from birth to adulthood. Interactions with parents, siblings, peers, and teachers will influence the pattern of behavior the child adopts.
2. From birth throughout the school years, every child needs unconditional love and feelings of security to develop into a healthy adult.
3. Every child needs to have experiences that allow growth opportunities to develop a positive self-concept.
4. Every child needs clear boundaries of acceptable behavior at home and at school.
5. Every child needs to learn autonomy as well as a sense of belonging and acceptance by parents, teachers, and peers.
6. Every child has the basic need to explore, to create, and to imagine.

7. Every child has the basic need to achieve and experience success.
8. Every child has a built-in sense of fairness and honesty.
9. Every child needs consistent guidance and discipline.
10. Every child can learn responsibility by developing an internal locus of control.
11. Every child can learn to self-correct inappropriate behavior.
12. No two children are alike in the manner in which they should be disciplined.

The individual situation, the child's history of behavior, socioeconomic background, and parental models all influence the manner in which a teacher or parent corrects a child.

Because of great variances in individual differences and environmental conditions, predicting specific behaviors is difficult. Children go through changes in behavior as they grow and develop. Teachers must always be cautious when examining any specific theory of development to explain a specific child's behavior. Basically, every educator has taught students who were different from the norm. Teachers must use professional judgment when working with students because no two students are exactly the same.

STUDENTS WITH DEVELOPMENTAL IMPAIRMENTS

As previously stated, the majority of students do not require major disciplinary action. During various stages of childhood, most children need to be guided in developing self-discipline. However, about 88% of students need only directions and clarification as they receive new information. The next 9% require additional corrective action but should not be considered developmentally impaired. The remaining 3% may have developmental impairments or be totally noncompliant.

Up to this point we have discussed normal development. Even within the normal range of development, kids will be kids and will require action for correction. However, normal students do not stop the instructional process. It is not normal for children to tell their teachers to "go to hell" or to walk out of the classroom. It is not normal for students to strike teachers or attack teachers with a knife. Of course, these examples are the most extreme, but any disruptive or unsafe behavior should be unacceptable, whether noncompliant behavior or behavior characteristic of a child with developmental impairments.

Children with developmental impairments usually come from a developmentally impaired family and have not had their developmental needs met in a healthy manner. They are therefore more likely to be withdrawn or noncompliant and have a tendency to be more aggressive and physical. To be successful, children with developmental impairments usually have to be controlled by an external source. The older the child, the less likely that teachers can succeed in promoting an internal locus of control. These children must learn obedience before they can learn responsibility.

Children with developmental impairments may emerge with the related unhealthy characteristics at any age. It is important to point out that these children are not necessarily attention deficit disordered or behaviorally impaired. Much is unknown about how young people sometimes develop in a negative framework. Children and adolescents with the most serious developmental impairments will be obvious because of acting-out behaviors. However, all teachers will have children with moderate developmental impairments who are not as obviously impaired. It is easy to overlook these students because they blend in with the normal achievers. In fact, many may be highly intelligent and high achievers. In spite of the fact that they are shy or do not act out, these students still have developmental impairments and need help and guidance.

SCHOOL DESIGN FOR PROMOTING STUDENT RESPONSIBILITY

In designing a school environment to enhance student responsibility, all faculty and staff must endorse the three principles of a responsibility-oriented school environment.

1. Schools must be for students—not principals and not teachers.
2. Students must be included in the decisions made to keep their school safe, clean, and inviting.
3. School curricula are adequately designed with placement of appropriate emphasis on academics, problem solving, and responsibility.

A principal described to us a situation he faced during his first year as principal.

> I recall a stressed-out teacher who came to my office near tears for an administrative team meeting one day. I can't recall her major concerns, but she ended her tirade with, "I could get something done if it weren't for some of my students." It hadn't been a particularly good day for me either. Still in my infancy as a principal, I responded to her charge by saying, "I could get something done if it were not for some of my teachers."

Needless to say, both individuals were frustrated. Perhaps they were stressed out because their needs were not met. Educators must recognize that addressing their own needs must be secondary to addressing the needs of students. Schools are for students. Schools administrators, teachers, and other staff members who believe differently have great difficulty in successfully meeting the educational outcomes central to the educational process.

Effective schools are safe. In a time of increased violence in American society and in schools, it is difficult to feel safe always. Doors cannot be locked to keep potentially disruptive students out of the building; however, several safety precautions can be implemented. Teachers can do the following:

- Report to the office any unidentified person on the school grounds. Visitors should wear an employee badge or a visitor's pass. Teach students to inform adults if they see anyone or anything out of the ordinary.
- Teach students safety procedures for working with any item, from scissors in kindergarten to chemicals and equipment in the twelfth grade. Review procedures at regular intervals.
- Review and practice fire, tornado, and other emergency drills and procedures on a regular basis.
- Integrate the teaching of safe habits into all areas of the instructional program, not just into health classes.
- Encourage the school system's administration to work with other local agencies to provide crossing guards, school police officers, and school nurses for all schools.

Effective schools are also clean. Sometimes it is difficult to get students to clean up their work spaces at school. However, with a little coaxing and reinforcement from teachers, things can get done. Teaching cleanliness should start at home. However, students generally do not lack knowledge of good hygiene and cleanliness, but, rather, they lack respect for either themselves, the school, or both. How can principals and teachers instill in students personal dignity for themselves and respect for school property?

Perhaps the first thing to be done at the school is to establish a Beautification Committee. To maximize success, consider the following:

- Committee members should include a school administrator, teachers, students, parents, and the head custodian.
- Students in the school must have ample opportunity to share their ideas and suggestions by having direct input into the decisions made concerning the school environment. School beautification contests can be held to solicit ideas from classes and individual students. The classes and students contributing the best suggestions should be recognized and given the opportunity to provide leadership in the implementation of their plans. All classes should be encouraged and expected to participate.
- PTAs can take on fund-raising projects to replace unsightly or damaged playground equipment or to plant trees, bushes, and flowers. If physical plant maintenance funding within the school system is limited, PTA members can initiate a classroom repainting project. Whatever the need may be, at all costs, keep

students directly involved, from planning stages through full implementation.

- At all grade levels, instruct students to keep desks, lockers, and cubbies clean and neat. On a weekly schedule, direct students in the cleaning of classroom and surrounding areas. This includes straightening materials and replacing misplaced items; dusting and washing desks, tables, and equipment in the room; and discarding clutter that has accumulated during the week. This will work well with elementary students. It is not cheap labor; it is allowing children to be responsible and have pride in themselves and their school. Older students enjoy decorating and personalizing their space. Let them act on their ideas. Perhaps clubs, grade levels, and classes can form teams to plan and share their ideas for cleaning and beautification.

- Encourage the school administration to place custodial staff on a shift schedule. The business community has been using this approach for years. It is difficult for custodians to clean the building during the school day. Custodial scheduling can be designed to have at least two shifts. For example, custodial support during the school day may be minimal for duties that must be performed at that time. The next shift of custodians can clean the building after school. At the system level, this concept can be expanded to include custodial teams who clean several schools a day after operating hours.

By following some of these recommendations, educators can maintain a safe and clean school. But schools must also be inviting, and not all safe and clean places are inviting. Everyone has eaten in a restaurant that was clean and safe, but where they felt out of place. If customers feel out of place and unwelcome, they probably do not go back. Students, however, obviously do not have the option of not returning to a school that is uninviting. If they were given a choice, they would elect to attend the school where they felt most comfortable, accepted, and invited. Until students gain that option, educators must make a collaborative effort with students to make the school environment more inviting. This requires a commitment at the classroom level and at the school level. Several suggestions that may help principals or teachers follow:

- Take inventory at a staff meeting of ideas for making the school a more inviting environment. It is important that faculty and staff feel invited, also. If a principal makes the request for ideas and the faculty do not respond, he or she could assume that they may be the obstacle to a warmer environment. With the risk of only a few bruises to their egos, principals can make healthy changes without losing authority. As former and practicing principals, we have found that the best way to improve morale and make the work environment more inviting is to empower responsible teachers to make responsible decisions.

- Much of what teachers view as inviting is also inviting for students. Just as a staff wants input into ways a school can be made more inviting, so does the student population. How can students learn responsibility and democracy if they are not allowed to be involved in the decision-making process? Anyone responding that students do not have this ability or will abuse the right has had limited experience working with children and youth or is closed-minded to true democracy and operates better in a dictatorial environment.

- Teachers and staff should dress professionally. Teachers should encourage and recognize appropriate dress for students. Students show a greater respect for a teacher who dresses as a responsible educator.

- Replace school rules with standards and guidelines. Regulations and rigid rules are considered uninviting by students and are frequently broken. Rules demand obedience. Rules do not foster the building of responsibility; rather, they dictate external control. With standards and guidelines, opportunity exists for flexibility in addressing situational differences. Obedience is required in some situations. However, rules are not always healthy or good for the students' well-being, because they enforce inflexibility or conformity. In contrast to rules, standards and guidelines give students ownership of their own behavior and permit them to develop responsibility or experience a self-correcting logical consequence. Some children may have difficulty because they have always been forced to be obedient and they have never been allowed to be responsible. For these students, teachers may need to initially alter the approach from a collaborative one to a more external-controlling environment until the students can establish an internally oriented classroom that fosters responsible behavior.

FOR REFLECTION

Designing a Warm and Inviting Environment

Take a minute to reflect on the elementary school that you attended as a student. What did you like about the school? Was it a warm, inviting place? If so, what made it inviting? If not, what made it uninviting?

THE RCM PLAN AND STUDENTS
WITH SPECIAL NEEDS

The RCM plan works well with most students having special needs. In fact, many teachers have commented that using the plan has made special needs classification of children less difficult because of the documentation procedures built into the model. Little or no adaptations need to be made in the model to accommodate most children with special needs. Students identified with attention deficit disorder, attention deficit hyperactivity disorder, physical disabilities, and learning disorders respond well to teachers using the RCM plan.

The research is conclusive in the area of addressing the behavior of behaviorally–emotionally disabled students. Teachers should never send children who have been certified as behaviorally–emotionally disabled to the Intensive Care Unit (described in Chapter 4). If these students are mainstreamed for part of their instruction and they become disruptive or hostile, teachers observing the behavior should follow the directions given in the child's individual education plan.

RESPONSIBILITY-ORIENTED CURRICULUM

Who determines what students are to learn in the school? Should developers of standardized tests or the publishers of textbooks dictate the curriculum? There are as many answers as there are people with different opinions, but one alternative is a curriculum that has responsibility as one of its major goals.

Society is composed of people. Although differences of race, sex, economic status, politics, religion, and philosophy are evident, citizens share basically a common culture. A common culture includes a heritage of knowledge, beliefs, values, and morals that is to be transferred from one generation to the next. This transfer is the process of education. Education is divided into two structures: informal and formal. In the informal structure, culture is transferred through parenting, religion, social interaction, and personal exploration. Much of this occurs before children enter school. However, informal learning continues during the school years when cultural transfer is accomplished through formal instruction. Through formal education, students gain cultural transfer through the process of schooling in public institutions. Educators often confuse the two types of education because of difficulty identifying which structure is responsible for the transfer of specific areas of the society's cultural heritage. Sex education exemplifies an area of such conflict. Additionally, citizens expect the school to be the panacea for the failure in the informal system of education, usually in parenting. Conversely, parents often enroll their child in a private school so that formal education can better parallel their informal education values. Many of these parents view public education as unreliable or irresponsible in preparing their child for adult life. Either way, the culture is transferred. However, the profession needs to clarify the boundaries. Although the teacher's role is to implement the curriculum through instruction, teachers need to unify efforts to limit educators' responsibility in the formal education process. In other words, formal education should be clearly defined in a documented form with specific outcomes. This documented form should be a written plan stating the specific outcomes or products that society expects. This is the written curriculum, written in a manner that provides reference points and guidelines for educators to follow in implementing the instructional process. In addition to academic outcomes, the curriculum must clearly define expectations for the development of responsible behavior. In previous decades, responsibility was taught within the informal structure. Today, society can no longer guarantee that this will occur. Instead, educators must demand that this become a major part of formal schooling.

Until society defines the limits and selects which goals schools are to achieve, the schools will continue to operate in a patchwork fashion. As a nation, citizens must clarify what product the schools are to cultivate and then demand that educators be given the freedom and resources to implement these. Until this happens, a patchwork system will continue to prevail, with inequality and inadequacy strongly influenced by the external control of lobbyists, interest groups, textbook publishers, test designers, and educators. School faculties must implement the present curriculum while striving to include application and problem-solving skills in every subject and program area. Teachers must accept the challenge to teach and demand that students practice the skills of responsible behavior.

The business community has become more interested in direct involvement in every aspect of the educational process. Employers know the importance of having well-educated and responsible employees in their organizations. Business–school partnerships will multiply rapidly during the 1990s. Financial assistance in the form of grants and projects is becoming more commonplace. Business community volunteers who provide instructional support to individuals and groups on the school grounds are solicited enthusiastically. Perhaps one of the most influential actions that a business organization can take is to allow educational leave time for employees to visit their children during the school day.

Educators must continue to experiment with alternative approaches to education. For example, experimentation with year-round schooling, evening programs, alternative training routes within the schools, and advancements in media and instructional technology to improve education will be commonplace. Another alternative is the move toward a nongraded, competency-based approach to learning. In this approach, students demonstrate mastery of a well-defined set of sequentially developed competencies based on developmentally appropriate factors. Requiring every student to complete educational levels at the same rate is limiting. Some children may master defined competencies in ten years, whereas other students may take fifteen years. Nobody fails in this approach. Students grow at their own pace and remain challenged and supported throughout the process. Critics may argue that this is financially unsound or socially damaging. Nothing is as financially unsound or socially damaging as the fact that 25% of the nation's youth are dropouts who are unemployed, living on the streets, or in prison as a result of the failure of society to educate them. As a society, Americans must find answers to these concerns. Accomplishments at the school level will have a lasting effect on the lives of all students. However, it is in the classroom where students really succeed or fail. It is in the classroom where teachers can have the most influence on students.

To promote student responsibility in the classroom, teachers must endorse the following principles:

1. Classrooms are student-centered.
2. Instruction is active and exciting.
3. Responsible behavior is learned and practiced.

Student-centeredness is more of an educational philosophy than an educational term. At some time in America's history, the belief that student-centered instruction places less academic challenge on the student emerged. If done correctly, no design is more rigorous. It is easy for teachers to recite content passively, often word for word, to obviously bored and frustrated students; but it is not instructionally sound. In activity-centered instruction, teachers discard the role of a passive content presenter and facilitate the development of a motivating and academically challenging environment for students through the use of activities during which students explore and learn through interactive experiences.

Following are several suggestions for establishing a student-centered classroom:

Set up the room in an attractive, warm, and inviting manner. Bulletin boards should have the work of last year's students displayed in a proud and boastful manner. Chairs, tables, and desks should be arranged so

FOR REFLECTION

If you were to write a description of the best teachers you had while in school, you would include the teachers who cared for you as a person and who made learning exciting. You may not remember all of the algebra, French, or geography taught, but you do remember the excitement and joy of being part of that particular class. Even a lecture can be active if effectively delivered.

that all students can see each other easily. This is difficult to do with straight rows. Teachers must be creative. Once students arrive, they must be permitted to have input into periodically changing the structure. Younger children will need more guidance in the beginning, and their arrangements may be unusual, to say the least. However, if teachers do not allow students to make these decisions, how can students learn to care for the classroom? Middle schools and secondary schools should have revolving committees of students that redesign the classroom environment monthly or quarterly. Classroom seating charts can be thrown away.

Display student artwork throughout the classroom. Teachers can bring a few nice plants and encourage students to bring plants. In addition, students must be allowed to keep selected personal items on their desks. A picture of a favorite pet or teenage idol can give a child a sense of home. Students spend half of their waking hours at school. Classrooms must belong to the kids.

Greet students in a caring and loving manner. Perhaps a statement such as, "Hi, Robert. I'm glad you are here today. I have an exciting experiment for us to do on . . . . " or "a story about . . . . " or "a game . . . . " Students always talk about how they love the first day of school. Educators must sustain that attitude through the remaining 179 days. If only every day in school had the excitement of the first day, there would be few school problems. Although everyone has good and bad days, teachers can make each day exciting. If every student had a teacher who said to her or him every day, "I'm glad you are here today," what an inviting world the schools would become. Behavior problems would be limited. Respect for teachers would increase. Authority is given, but respect must be earned. Educators who forget this basic premise are doomed to fail, and so are their students.

Interact with students and get to know them. Be assertive in becoming informed about students' personal lives. When teachers ask the right questions, the most they will have to do is to listen. Consider sharing a little of your personal self on a regular basis. The recounting of an experience in the grocery store or a predicament a son experiences will show students that a teacher's life doesn't revolve solely around the classroom. Direct conversational time between children and adults on a daily basis has dropped dramatically in recent decades. As teachers talk with children, they need to suggest multiple avenues to explore in solving problems or investigating ideas. That is the good part of the learning process. Educators must avoid being preachy and excessively corrective. Teach by example. When teachers do this, students learn that teachers care for them as whole beings. Children and youth have a natural propensity toward truth and fairness if they have not been damaged developmentally. Caring teachers will gain their respect. Students who respect their teachers will not exhibit major behavior problems. However, teachers must keep in mind that to

Interact with students and get to know them.

gain a student's respect, they do not have to be personal friends or buddies. In fact, that can be damaging to the integrity of the relationship. Yet doing the things a caring teacher does is imperative. Teachers have a great responsibility in the instructional process. A master teacher knows when to reprimand, to hug, to counsel, and to listen. Occasionally, educators make mistakes. That is natural. Children are most forgiving when they know the mistakes are not intentional and the mistakes are acknowledged. Everyone makes mistakes as they grow. Stagnation is not growth.

Design a classroom environment where responsible behaviors are learned and reinforced daily. Responsible behavior demonstrates a value of the principles of honesty, morality, and commitment. Responsible people are accountable for their actions and accept that with any action there is a natural consequence. Responsible behavior begins at home as children learn by modeling their parents. Children chart their futures according to the resolution of early conflicts. Whether teachers assist or hinder children's efforts to resolve these conflicts and develop responsible behavior will depend on how they model responsible behavior to students and how they monitor socially appropriate and inappropriate behavior with respect to standards and guidelines.

INSTRUCTIONAL IDEAS

Teachers can include concepts about responsibility into the instructional program at the elementary, middle, and secondary levels in numerous ways. Some examples follow:

Elementary School, Middle School, and Secondary School

Spend the first week in all classes discussing various aspects of responsibility. For example, in the area of social studies at all grade levels, the concept of responsibility can be interwoven into nearly any unit of study.

Middle School and Secondary School

Design an instructional bulletin board where students can post their drawings, cartoons, essays, etc., on the topic of responsible behavior. Put up a graffiti board where students can write or draw ideas and concerns.

Upper Elementary Grades, Middle School, and Secondary School

Let the class write songs, poems, letters, and essays related to responsibility, citizenship, and civility.

Elementary School and Middle School

Use grade-level literature in which students can relate to characters and can identify concepts of responsibility, behavior, and consequences.

Middle School and Secondary School

Develop a Wanted Poster hall, bulletin board, chart, or graffiti area, and let students write what they think their behavior must be for them to be responsible students, good citizens, and/or productive members of society.

Use literature to model and role-play responsible behavior.

PUTTING CONCEPTS INTO PRACTICE

Class Activity

As a class or in a group, make a list of other activities teachers can do to teach responsibility.

Questions for Discussion and Related Activities

1. Respond to the following quote: "Discipline is the student's responsibility."

2. Think of one or two of your teachers when you were in school who seldom had any discipline problems. Write down some qualities or characteristics of these teachers. What did these teachers do to avoid discipline problems? After a few minutes of individual recording, get into small groups and share responses. While in groups, come up with five teacher behaviors that are common in the group, and have a recorder write these on the board or a chart. Common responses may include high expectations, did not threaten but acted, cared for the students, was honest and direct, used active instructions, student involvement was high, or expected responsible behavior.

3. Are any of the behaviors collected in activity 2 appropriate for schools today? Which will be appropriate in ten years?

4. Select a student to stand near the board and record students' responses to the questions, "What is a responsible student?" "What behaviors do responsible students exhibit?"

5. Discuss in a large group the responsibility level of the students in the schools today. What can be done to make these students more responsible for their actions?

6. Examine the three major types of disciplinary approaches that have been used with students in the past: brute technique, rules technique, and the paper child technique. Make a list under each technique of specific examples or situations that students in the past have experienced from teachers in the classroom at the elementary, middle, and high school levels. How would these lists compare to the techniques teachers use today in the schools? In the future?

7. Review the developmental aspects of behavior. Complete this review with a discussion of the child with developmental impairments. Discuss the 88%, 9%, and 3% indicators of behavior found in the research.

8. Working individually, describe ten ways the schools can be made cleaner, safer, and more inviting. Next, develop a plan of how you can make the classroom cleaner, safer, and more inviting.

REFERENCES

Elam, S. M., Rose, L. C., & Gallup, A. M. (1992). The twenty-fourth annual Gallup/Phi Delta Kappa poll of the public's attitudes toward the public schools. *Phi Delta Kappan, 74,* 41–53.

U.S. Department of Education. (1983). *A nation at-risk: the imperatives of educational reform.* National Commission on Excellence in Education. Washington, DC: U.S. Government Printing Office.

U.S. Department of Education. (1991). *America 2000: an education strategy.* Washington, DC: U.S. Government Printing Office.

U.S. Department of Education. (1994). *Goals 2000: Educate america act.* Washington, DC: U.S. Government Printing Office.

Young, M. A. (1993). National priorities for education: a conversation with U.S. Secretary of Education, Richard W. Riley. *National Forum, 73*(4), 5–7.

SUGGESTED READINGS

Kohn, A. (1991). Caring kids: The role of the schools. *Phi Delta Kappan, 73,* 496–506.

Kohn, A. (1993). Choices for children: Why and how to let students decide. *Phi Delta Kappan, 75*(1), 8–19.

Kohn, A. (1993). *Punished by rewards: The trouble with gold stars, incentive plans, "As", praise, and other bribes.* Boston: Houghton Mifflin.

Purkey, W. W., & Novak, J. M. (1984). *Inviting school success* (2nd ed.). Belmont, CA: Wadsworth.

Purkey, W. W., & Queen, J. A. (1985). Seven gifts for the beginning teacher. *Focus on Learning, 11*(1), 105–108.

Purkey, W. W., & Straham, D. (1989). *Positive discipline: A pocketful of ideas.* Columbus, OH: National Middle School Association.

Implementing
the RCM Plan

STANDARDS AND GUIDELINES VERSUS RULES

Take a few moments to answer the following questions with *yes* or *no*:

1. While driving on the highway, have you ever traveled more than the posted speed limit?
2. In school did you ever cheat on an exam or school work?
3. Did you ever fail to report on your taxes money you earned that was paid to you in cash?
4. While employed as a teacher, have you ever taken or used school property for personal use?
5. In paying your bills, have you ever mailed a check without appropriate funds in your account to cover the check?
6. When asked about a delayed payment or a letter that should have been received, have you ever responded that it was mailed and placed blame on the postal system when, in fact, it had not been sent?
7. Have you ever kept money from a clerk's error in giving you more change than was owed?
8. Did you ever bump or scratch a parked car and not report the damage?
9. At work have you ever come in late or left early without the principal's permission?
10. Have you ever told someone that you were sick when you really were not sick?

While answers of *yes* to any of these questions may not label one as a convict, there is a point to be made. Although most people have broken some of the rules, most people are basically moral individuals. Then why are rules broken? Better still, when are rules broken? As members of society, individuals break rules when they think the rules are senseless or inappropriate. People break rules when they are either in need or have a limited fear of getting caught. For example, Mr. Jones is late leaving work and needs to get home. No highway patrol officers are in sight, so he exceeds the speed limit to make up for lost time. Another example might be when he goes to the movies instead of completing the unpleasant task of scoring the sixty essays that he promised to return the next day and then tells his students a brief illness prevented him from finishing. Responsibility can be measured by degree. For instance, someone who answered *no* to all of the preceding questions may be viewed as more responsible than someone who answered *no* to only five of the ten questions. Actions are directly related to how one measures right and wrong. Value structure directs one's level of responsibility.

REPLACING RULES WITH STANDARDS

Rules, whether written or implied, place restraints on individuals as members of a free society. Most people basically do not like rules, but boundaries are important. With no boundaries, chaos results. Children and youth also need boundaries. Without healthy boundaries, children do not feel safe and they do not develop normally. However, rules are absolute. Rules imply rigidity and equal treatment. Everyone is not treated equally, however. In American society, equality—at least to some degree—is determined by birthright or by the socioeconomic structure in which a child lives. The myth that all a child has to do to gain equality is to get an education lives on.

Yet educators design an educational environment that does not compensate for individual differences or accommodate values outside of the middle-class value system. Therefore, a majority of students learn to follow the rules as long as the authority figure is monitoring. These students learn externally enforced obedience that does not teach a true sense of responsibility. Some students actively resist an environment that is alien to their way of life or that cannot accommodate their dysfunctions. In schools today, educators often attack the freedom and individuality that are the basic cornerstones of the nation. In other words, teachers attack the dignity of students or go to the opposite extreme and bribe students into achieving or behaving. Discipline must be taught and practiced in a way that allows students their dignity. Teachers can learn to discipline with respect and without the overemphasized fear that curbs the positive development of self-esteem. Children who have become award addicts also may have a self-esteem problem.

In Chapter 3, we stated that teachers have to be responsible adults if they are to teach responsibility to students. This is paramount to the success of this program. To use the Responsible Classroom Management (RCM) plan, teachers may have to modify some of their teaching behaviors. Listed below are the major behaviors that we believe a teacher must practice to succeed:

1. Replace rules with democratic standards and guidelines.
2. Use directives to state desirable student behavior.
3. Expect responsible behavior from all students.

If teachers have been using a model of classroom management that focuses on rules, they will have some difficulty in making the transition to standards and guidelines. However, once the change is made, student management will be more effective and less stressful. Rules are destined to be broken, at least in part, by just about everyone. Only one's own value system will determine to what degree. If an individual's value system has been influenced by focused rules and tight authority, one tends to develop a sense of obedience. At times, obedience is appropriate—even lifesaving. However, for citizens in a free society, responsibility is more democratic. Responsibility can be learned best in a democratic setting that allows for individualism and the opportunity for self-correction. A system that uses standards and guidelines can achieve best what as a profession teachers desire: responsible students who grow up to be responsible adults.

STANDARDS, GUIDELINES, AND DIRECTIVES

In the RCM plan, rules are not used. Instead, the teacher uses standards, guidelines, and directives. *Standards* define the general direction of the responsible behavior. *Guidelines* provide specific guidance toward successfully meeting those standards. *Directives* are used to give specific statements of expected behaviors, usually for safety reasons. Directives require certain specific behaviors because safety is the most important factor. Not following the directive can result in the natural consequence of the action, sometimes harmful or injurious in nature. For example, "Justin, don't play in the road" is a directive. For better effect, a directive should be stated in negative form for extremely dangerous situations, and possible consequences should be included. For example, "Justin, don't play in the road because you could get hit by a car and be badly hurt." Stating the directive in this form takes some of the mystery out of the command. Stating a directive without the possible negative consequence may generate curiosity in children to take action to find out why. Some children may be motivated to test the consequence even when it is specifically stated. For example, "Boys and girls, this is an electric pencil sharpener. Please do not put your finger in the pencil hole because the blade can cut your finger." If students still fail to follow the directive, limitations are placed on their behavior.

Directives are important because they allow responsible adults a mechanism for guiding children in safe, responsible behavior. Directives are used more frequently in the lower grades, where children have limited experience in making safe and appropriate decisions. However, these children learn that the directive stated with a specific and related consequence is something that they do not want to test. This is one of the first signs of growing responsibility. Why? Because the consequence is directly voiced. Children learn that the teacher places their welfare at the heart of the directive. The specificity of the consequence description allows them to visualize the danger. Another element can be added to the directive to better humanize it, "Boys and girls, this is an electric pencil sharpener. Please do not put your finger in the pencil hole because the blades could hurt your finger. I don't want you to get hurt." Directives are repeated often when the greatest possibility of danger exists. For example, mothers direct preschoolers every time they go outside to play not to go into the road. In time children will, hopefully, internalize and accept the directive as their own: they don't go into the road because they don't want to get hit by a car and get hurt. Later, they will develop skills to walk on the road safely and carefully.

Directives can also be used in procedural areas of instruction. For example, in biology class, certain procedures are necessary for dissecting a frog. Students not following the directive that states specific procedures may end up with an unusable specimen. Procedures stated as directives can expedite certain tasks. For example, "Please have your lunch money on your tray as you go to the cashier so the cashier can pick it up quickly. This allows the line to move faster so that you have more time for lunch." In this case, a positive consequence is stated. Again, a directive is stated directly to individuals or groups and has the consequence built directly into the statement. Care for the students' well-being is most important. Directives can be repeated regularly until the process is internalized.

Notice that no punishments are stated. Punishment for these behaviors is not natural and will have a short-term effect. For example, if a parent threatens to spank her child if he goes into the road, the child may be obedient as long as his mother is watching, simply out of fear of being spanked. The child may not discover the real danger of the road, because the emphasis on the behavior was the fear of punishment. When the parent turns away, this child is in more danger because he may not sense the care for him and does not internalize the impending danger. This child may remain obedient and operate out of fear of punishment, or he may be motivated to go into the road if he thinks his parents are not looking. A directive is more effective. In addition to the advantages of the directive already discussed, use of the directive provides opportunity for teachers to exercise professional judgment in stating directives to meet the needs of students. Directives may be modified to meet specific needs.

The professional judgment of teachers or principals is used in issuing directives. Directives are used to assist children to perform what are considered by society to be responsible behaviors. If students respect their teachers, they will be more apt to follow teachers' directives. As students develop increased responsibility, most directives can be replaced with only an occasional reminder. As students develop and internalize appropriately stated directives, many of the directives will become unnecessary. For example, "You don't play in the road" becomes internalized and unnecessary as a directive.

Just as directives can also be used to meet specific procedural requirements, standards are used to formalize social and academic expectations. Standards are cooperatively designed by students and staff. Examples of some standards that may be used follow:

1. I am responsible for all of my actions.
2. My success is directly related to my effort.
3. To achieve in life I must get an education.

These are just a few examples. However, the number of standards should be kept to a minimum; no more than two standards should be used on a schoolwide or classroom basis. The most effective schools have used only one standard for the entire school. By far the most successful standard is, *"I am responsible for all my actions at Smith Elementary School."*

With standards, there are always guidelines. Younger students will need more input from teachers in determining guidelines than older students. Guidelines provide guidance to students in harmony with the standard. The role of teachers is to make sure the guidelines are educationally sound and fair, but these should be developed mutually by students and teachers.

Classroom standards may or may not be the same as the school standards. However, the school standards, which are practiced schoolwide, should be incorporated into the classroom program. As mentioned, the most successful schools have used only one standard for the school and all of the classrooms. This is less confusing to students and staff and enables teachers to ensure that standards are followed consistently.

School guidelines for hall behavior and lunchroom behavior, respect, and other schoolwide issues can be used in the RCM plan. Specific guidelines for each classroom or grade level must be developed for optimum success. These guidelines must guide and support school standards. School standards must be posted throughout the school in several visible places.

Be sure to involve students in the planning of classroom guidelines.

Maximizing Benefits of the RCM Plan

For the best results, educators and students (usually class or grade representatives) collaborate to develop one major schoolwide standard, which also serves as the classroom standard. Next, the group develops school guidelines for areas outside the classroom. Classroom guidelines are designed by classroom teachers and students. Guidelines can also be developed by grade levels in a team approach, a method found most often in the middle schools.

A classroom guideline might be, "To be a responsible student in sixth grade, I will be a good team member by treating all of my teachers and peers with genuine respect."

Classroom Guidelines

Classroom guidelines should be posted in the classroom and taught to the students with discussion and role playing as accompaniment. For example, the standard "I am responsible for all of my actions" will have different expectations for kindergarten students from those for older students. In addition, when possible, state the standard in a positive fashion. Guidelines always begin with "I," or more effectively, "To be a responsible student in the third grade, I will . . . . " Note the examples shown in Figure 4–1.

Responsible behavior for responsible people in a responsible society is a major emphasis of the RCM plan. If all educators use this approach, the vast majority of students will not exhibit inappropriate behaviors. Teachers need to keep expectations positive and developmentally appropriate for best results. Teaching should become a joy again.

What about the 9% of students who require increased correction and the developmentally impaired 3%? If teachers implement the RCM plan as stated so far, the percentage of students requiring disciplinary action may not be as high as 12%. However, the answer to the question is to allow for logical consequences to occur for students who have difficulty adhering to standards, guidelines, and teacher directives.

USING LOGICAL CONSEQUENCES

All students will occasionally need reminders to correct behavior. However, responsible students will develop an internal locus of control, which will allow them to develop self-correcting mechanisms. Sometimes, students with minor problems only need someone to listen and to offer guidance. Many times, teachers work with students who need only occasional redirection. However, teachers may not work as effectively with children who have chronic behavior problems. Teachers must work with all students and, therefore, must develop strategies to avoid major pitfalls that could hinder their

FIGURE 4–1
Example of an RCM School Standard and Guidelines

School Standard
As a student at Smith Middle School, I am responsible for all of my actions.

School Guideline
Any serious or repetitive act of student behavior that disrupts the normal educational process is considered irresponsible behavior.

Second Grade Guidelines
To be responsible in second grade, I will . . .
1. Respect myself, other students, and school property.
2. Put forth my best effort with a positive attitude.

Sixth Grade Guidelines
To be responsible in sixth grade, I will . . .
1. Come to class with appropriate materials and be prepared to learn.
2. Participate in class activities with a positive attitude.

Ninth Grade Guidelines
To be a responsible student in ninth grade, I will . . .
1. Come to school prepared to learn.
2. Treat myself, others, and school property with respect.

Eleventh Grade Guidelines
To be a responsible student in eleventh grade, I will . . .
1. Come to class with appropriate materials and preparation and with an attitude appropriate for learning.
2. Assist the teacher in making learning exciting and challenging every day.

---

effectiveness with all students. Before using logical consequences with students for inappropriate behavior, teachers must make sure that they have not created the problem(s) by stumbling into one or more of the following pitfalls:

1. Promising students that if they complete a task they will receive a treat.
2. Arguing with a student of any age over any problem.
3. Becoming emotional when correcting students.
4. Raising their voice level above the normal range.
5. Praising students when praise is undeserved.
6. Giving rewards to get appropriate behavior.
7. Embarrassing or belittling students.
8. Using inappropriate language with students, such as *shut up, dumb, or pathetic.*
9. Treating students unfairly.
10. Planning ineffectively for instruction.

There are more than the ten pitfalls listed, but these are the major ones. When teachers stumble into one or more of these common pitfalls, students and teachers suffer. The use of fear of punishment or threat of coercion can achieve some degree of obedient behavior or short-range control, but it is temporary and ineffective in teaching responsibility. It is sad to hear teachers boast that they have punished a child for inappropriate behavior. They may have gotten rid of the behavior problem for a short time, but they probably have lost the child. It does not make sense. Teachers must learn to balance management of student behavior with respect for the self-esteem of the individual child. Teachers have a right and a responsibility to teach. Children have a right to an education, but they also have a responsibility not to interfere with the learning of other students. Pitfalls are easy to avoid if teachers remain responsible and professional. Most of the pitfalls listed are self-explanatory; however, in the following discussion, we elaborate on a few.

Some children are easily intimidated by threatening teachers who shout to maintain order. These students may never feel any partnership or ownership of their class, because they are always on guard for an attack from their teachers. Students must feel at ease to work to their potential. Teachers must feel at ease with their authority in the classroom to be effective in the management of student behavior. Teachers who argue with a student lose. Teachers do not have to argue or tolerate unacceptable behav-

Students can be taught to solve their problems.

ior. Arguing with students does not improve unacceptable behavior. It only places teachers within the control of the students. Older students will do almost anything, including arguing, to avoid losing face among their peers. Nobody wins in this situation.

Students create more problems within the classroom when they are bored or confused. The majority of behavior problems in the classroom can be eliminated by implementing active instructional strategies and by including interactive activities in the instructional program. Students who are motivated and are engaged in their learning have little time for misbehavior. They also have much greater respect for their teachers. Teachers who are highly respected have few behavior problems at any grade level or in any subject.

Teachers often use rewards as bribery for good behavior. This is an external controlling mechanism that focuses student attention on gaining the reward, not on establishing responsible behavior. Students become dependent on rewards as an external stimulation to accomplish a task. The effects of rewards are only short-lived and do not encourage responsible performance without a repeat of the reward. However, teachers should encourage, acknowledge, and affirm student achievement and appropriate behavior.

What do teachers need to do when directives are not followed and guidelines are broken? Teachers need to limit the opportunity for the recurrence of the behavior and need to allow students to experience the logical consequences.

Logical consequences link inappropriate student action to a specific guideline. Logical consequences are not punishment. These actions are a natural result of not doing what is expected. For example, one guideline states that students will come to school prepared to learn. In discussing what is to be expected in this guideline, teachers give a directive that students complete a specific homework assignment. Every child is expected to do the homework. Students who come in without their homework are not penalized with a low grade. Instead, they are asked when they would like to complete the assignment—at break, during lunch, or after school. What happens if the same children do not have their homework in the future? The same or a similar consequence is used. In another example, children are throwing food in the cafeteria. A logical consequence is that these students sit by the teacher or alone until they choose to act responsibly in the cafeteria. Only a rebellious student will create a scene over the enforcement of this logical consequence.

It is important that the setting for permitting a logical consequence be private and professional. For example, when teachers discuss with students the consequences of not doing their homework, they should show no emotional reaction, either verbally or nonverbally. Sometimes, students have a reasonable explanation for a certain behavior. The teacher should always listen to the reason. However, patterns must be identified. For example, a teacher gives a directive that all students going on a class field trip must return a permission form signed by a parent/guardian. On the day of the field trip, a fourth grader has not returned the field trip permission form, which was given to him three days earlier. He explains that his mother signed it and inadvertently placed it in her briefcase. His mother is out of town on a business trip but calls the teacher long distance at the last minute and explains the situation. What will most teachers do? Will the student be held accountable and not allowed to go? Or will the teacher vary the consequence? Before finalizing the consequence, the teacher may want to consider the following questions. Did the teacher give adequate time for return of the signed permission form? Is the student old enough to be expected to ensure that the form be returned? If not, was he reminded after the first or second day? Consequences should be reasonable and fair for the student at this particular age and stage of development. Although children should not be penalized for the actions of their parents, teachers do children no favors when overlooking actions that are well within their control. In this case, the student had three days to return the form. A logical consequence of not allowing the student to go would obviously correct the behavior. The student will not forget the form in the future.

Teachers should have several consequences available for any inappropriate action. The more logical consequences that one has available, the more effective the teacher will be in addressing any specific situation. *Being fair to students does not always mean treating students the same.* Every situation differs. Students come from a variety of backgrounds and situations. A consequence for one student for a behavior over which he or she has little control may be inappropriate for a student having more control. Most inappropriate behavior can be measured in degrees—so can appropriate, logical consequences.

Consequences may also be assigned in the form of time-out. Time-out should be a logical consequence of an inappropriate action. For example, in a first-grade class during a reading activity, a child pushes another child in an attempt to get her to play. The teacher directs the misbehaving child to stop the disruptive activity. If the child continues to push, the teacher can choose the time-out option for the child. This is an appropriate use of time-out because it is being used to remove the child from the disruptive activity. It provides the child with an opportunity to refocus her attention while allowing the learning process to continue unimpeded for the other students. Time-out is not appropriate in RCM if it is used as a

F O R   R E F L E C T I O N

Think back to a time when you misbehaved in school. How did the teacher respond? What may have been a more acceptable response?

form of punishment. For example, a child who does not have his home-work should not be placed in time-out. Time-out is not a logical conse-quence for not doing homework.

Children can be assigned to time-out in the classroom or in a col-league's classroom. Partnerships with other teachers for time-out periods can be quite successful. Time-out is not a punishment for the misbehavior. It is an opportunity for children to refocus their energy into a more appro-priate behavior. To tell a six-year-old child that she is placed in time-out for twenty minutes makes the action a punishment. Instead, the teacher uses the time to monitor the student. The desire is for the student to say that she is ready to return to the group. This might occur in three minutes or in eight. If she does not ask to return to the group, it is the teacher's responsi-bility to ask her if she is ready to return. If the student asks to return before the teacher asks her and she follows instructions as directed, then she has begun to accept responsibility for her actions. It may take more than one time, but it will work.

Time-out is not recommended as a consequence in the classroom structure beyond fourth grade. It is most effective in preschool and early elementary grades. However, students at any age who are extremely disrup-tive can be *isolated* in a predetermined space for an extensive period of time until they agree to come back to the classroom and act responsibly. Teachers should use this in the most serious situations such as those involving continuous, extremely disruptive behavior.

The average length of stay in time-out before the teacher approaches the child about readiness to return to instruction should average about one to one and one-half minutes per year of age of the child. However, if the child expresses that he is not ready to rejoin the group after the suggested maxi-mum amount of time, the teacher may wish to use another consequence.

Another example of logical consequences is the Freeze Technique, which is detailed in Figure 4–2. The Freeze Technique can be used with elementary and middle school students who habitually refuse to do any class work.

What if students become hostile or refuse to accept the consequences of their actions or continue to experience ineffective consequences? Those students may need to be temporarily removed from the class and placed in an intensive care situation.

THE INTENSIVE CARE UNIT

Similar to hospitalized patients who require more than routine nursing care and are sent to the Intensive Care Unit (ICU) for closer monitoring, stu-

FIGURE 4–2

The Freeze Technique

1. The student is informed that he or she is not being responsible.

2. Parents are sent a letter informing them that their child is not participating and that after numerous attempts to get the child involved, you have decided to spend time with students wishing to learn. As soon as the child decides to be part of the class, you will assist that student in any way possible to ensure academic success. Tell the parents they will be informed on a weekly basis of their child's status.

3. Place a chart with the names of students on Freeze somewhere visible in the room.

4. Record in some manner every time that work is not completed. This can be done by keeping the number of assignments not completed or by using greater detail.

5. Refuse to give the student any attention, especially negative attention. Remember, you have been getting zero. Why waste your energy and let other students suffer? The student is presently refusing to work whether you react or not.

6. Once the student begins doing any work, positively encourage and unfreeze.

7. Remove the student's name from the group list when the child completes all work for a week.

8. Continue Freeze three to six weeks for any student not fully participating in class activities and assignments.

9. If after six weeks improvement is not noted, refer the student for social or emotional assistance. Students do not normally behave in this manner. Something is wrong.

10. Be consistent. The only way to reverse this problem in the classroom is to withhold all attention until desirable behavior begins. The goal is to change the behavior by changing the type of attention the student receives—from negative attention, to no attention, to positive attention. These students want attention. If they get only negative attention, they will continue on the present path, because negative attention is better than no attention. If they begin to receive no attention, their need for attention will be difficult to resist. They will soon realize that it is better to do the work and get positive attention than no attention.

11. Almost universally, a student who is being "Freezed" will act out in class initially because the need for attention is so great. If this occurs, the student should be sent to the ICU immediately. This student should remain in the ICU for a much longer period of time, up to two to three hours if necessary.

dents who do not respond appropriately to other consequences prescribed within the classroom can be monitored outside the classroom. No longer should teachers tolerate misbehavior that students elect not to correct.

Planning Ahead for the ICU

Intensive care will work only when a principal or an administrative team is supportive and directly involved. Teachers will no longer need to send students to the office for misbehavior when they use the following recommendations to develop an effective ICU.

1. Before school starts, the ICU setting must be established and the tone must be set. The ideal environment for intensive care is a small classroom or mobile unit that has been equipped with a selection of desks, chairs, and tables of various sizes to accommodate students of different ages. The room is to be a safe, supervised area.

2. Paperwork for tracking use of the ICU and documentation and parent reporting of this intervention technique are developed as part of the preparation for ICU. Suggested forms are listed in Appendixes A and B.

3. The administrative team develops a schedule for supervision of students who are placed in intensive care. The team should enlist the assistance of teacher assistants, administrative assistants, teachers, counselors, office clerks, and closely screened adult volunteers.

4. Arrangements must be made for the intensive care area to be monitored by two adults in shifts of forty-five to ninety minutes. Intensive care should be available from school opening until the end of the school day. The monitors in the room serve two functions: to supervise and to record student responses to what happened in the classroom, hallway, and so on.

Using the ICU Correctly

Robert is in Mrs. Smith's fourth-grade class. Apparently, Robert had a difficult morning before coming to school. Mrs. Smith has already given two consequences to Robert for breaking two guidelines. Because the present environment is not effective for Robert at this time, she decides to send Robert to the ICU. Quietly and without emotional display, she sends Robert to the ICU. The motive is not to embarrass Robert or to confront him at this time about his behavior. The motive is to address the inappropriate behavior with the least possible disruption to instruction. Mrs. Smith informs the office. The office then notifies the intensive care monitor, who goes to the classroom and directs Robert to follow her to the ICU. Various systems can be used to notify the ICU that a student needs to be admitted.

When Robert enters the ICU, he is immediately assigned a seat and directed to sit quietly until a monitor can talk with him. Once available, the monitor sits down with Robert and simply asks him what has happened during the past thirty minutes. If Robert elects to talk, the monitor listens, making no comment and displaying no judgment either verbally or nonverbally. Robert has the choice of not talking and has to sit quietly until Mrs. Smith can come to the ICU to talk to him.

Our research shows that the ICU is more effective if no work is assigned to students while they are in the ICU. The goal is to help the student refocus and receive guidance and direction from the teacher before returning to class. Unsolicited talking or disruptive behavior in the ICU by a student results in immediate intervention by the principal or the principal's designee.

Taking care not to interrupt instruction, Mrs. Smith arrives at the ICU at her earliest convenience. She sits down with Robert and resolves the issue in a caring, but firm manner. Once Mrs. Smith is convinced that Robert has resolved the problem and has his behavior under control, he returns to the classroom. Mrs. Smith completes a form that describes the inappropriate behavior, explains the responsible behavior that is expected of Robert, and details how the situation was resolved. This form should remain simple but provide adequate information. A copy of the document is given to the monitor for filing in the office, and another is mailed to the parent. If Robert refuses to correct his behavior or talks and acts out during intensive care, he remains there until the principal or assistant principal is available to intervene.

Basic Questions and Answers About ICUs

Q: How long should a behavior be tolerated in the classroom before the misbehaving child is placed in intensive care?

A: In the preceding scenario, Robert may have been having problems for two or three days before he was sent to intensive care, or his inappropriate behavior may have occurred two minutes before he was removed from the room. A formula is hard to use. The basic point to remember is that no child has the right to interfere with the learning of another.

Q: What is the recommended maximum length of a stay in the ICU?

A: There are no time limits for stays in intensive care. The length of time a child remains is determined by the teacher, a professional capable of making responsible decisions. The teacher's professional judgment and care for the student should weigh heavily in determining an effective length of stay. In higher grade levels, a full-time person may be hired to monitor the ICU, counsel the student, and complete the forms.

Q: Should a student be expected to complete work missed while in the ICU?

A: This must be left up to the individual teacher, who bases the decision on the needs of the child. The child's age, complexity of work missed, and the teacher's time should be factors examined. Note: Be aware that some children may discover that they can use the ICU to avoid class work. The teacher obviously will require those children to make up the work or will not use the ICU for them.

Q: Most of the preceding questions focus more on the child in elementary school or self-contained middle-grade classrooms. How does ICU work for team situations, departmentalized settings, or the secondary school?

A: Procedures are somewhat similar with respect to forms and supervision. Some secondary schools and some elementary schools use a team approach: Teachers, administrators, parents, and students serve on the Discipline Review Committee (DRC). The structure and function of the DRC are presented in detail in Chapter 5. However, with respect to the ICU, teachers usually serve as ICU supervisors on a rotational basis. Because older students have more than two or three teachers, sometimes when a student is sent to ICU, the supervisory teacher writes up the ICU report and sends documents to the necessary people. After a student is sent to the ICU a second time, the DRC monitors the process. The complete process is presented in Chapter 5 in the discussion of middle and secondary models.

Q: What if intensive care does not work for a student and the teacher does not want to enlist the assistance of the principal at this time? What else can be tried?

A: To complement the intensive care model, the teacher can use a Behavior Improvement Agreement with the child.

BEHAVIOR IMPROVEMENT AGREEMENTS

Teacher Behavior Improvement Agreement

Several options are available in using the Behavior Improvement Agreement (BIA). This agreement can be used by classroom teachers as an instrument *if intensive care does not work or if intensive care is not available in the school.* Therefore, the agreement can be used in the classroom by teachers using the RCM plan independently. The agreement can be used as the final step before the problem is brought to the attention of a school administrator.

When a teacher decides to use the BIA, the teacher informs the student that all other attempted approaches toward correction of the undesirable behavior have not been successful. If the student agrees, the plan is the final approach the teacher will use before turning the problem over to the principal. This plan differs from the social contract and academic contract that are used for groups or individuals to reward achievement or manage instruction. The agreement approach in the RCM plan is the final attempt to improve behavior before major corrective action occurs. The teacher and the student together list improper behaviors that must be discontinued. This is most effective when the descriptions of improvement needed are written in the student's own words. Next, the teacher writes the consequences that will occur if the contractual promises are broken. In the teacher–student agreement, there may be just one consequence—a conference with an administrative team member. Another appropriate consequence for teacher use is a mandatory parent conference. Note that the approval of a school administrator must be obtained before initiating this consequence. The student signs the agreement, and the teacher sends one copy to the child's parents and gives another copy to the child. The teacher keeps the original. A copy of the agreement is also filed in a special file in the school office. If no agreement is reached, the principal is notified. An example of a completed BIA form appears in Figure 4–3.

Q: If intensive care was not effective, and the behavior contract was broken, what should the teacher do?

A: The child's teacher is the best judge. Again, formulas are not the best approach. Teachers must be certain that intensive care is not being used as punishment or as a means only to get a student out of the class. The BIA should be fair and appropriate. However, teachers should not tolerate inappropriate behavior from students. To tolerate inappropriate behavior is unfair to the teacher, to the other students in the class, and to the child who is engaging in irresponsible behavior. If the teacher determines that intensive care or the BIA has not been effective for a student, then it is the teacher's responsibility to inform the principal.

Principal Behavior Improvement Agreement

A school administrator or a team of teachers who serve on the DRC can use the BIA as a final instrument before suspension. The agreement has the same three components, regardless of when it is used. The components include promised behaviors, consequences, and the signatures of the parties involved.

In designing an agreement, the principal may use the conditions developed by the teacher and add stronger consequences. The principal can use this approach for students who have not been successful in intensive care or for those students who have delivered threats or acted abusively toward other students and faculty. The agreement format is the same. However, we suggest that the principal have two or three consequences, which might include therapeutic time-out from school, suspension, or legal

FIGURE 4–3
Teacher-Prepared Model BIA

BEHAVIOR IMPROVEMENT AGREEMENT
TEACHER

Robert D. _____   Mr. J _____
Student   Homeroom Teacher

0054321 _____   Mrs. L. _____
ID. #   Recommending Teacher

6th _____   11-7-97 _____
Grade/Class   Date

PROMISED BEHAVIORS

I, Robert D _____ **agree** and **promise** to do the following:

1.) To keep my hands and feet to myself and avoid hitting, kicking,
    or striking anyone at school;

2.) To not use profanity or vulgarity in any form while at school.

Failure to keep this agreement will result in the issuance of the following
consequences:

CONSEQUENCES

A.) A mandatory conference with parents before returning to class;
    AND/OR

B.) Reported to the principal.

SIGNATURES

Robert D. _____   Mrs. L _____
Student   Teacher

---

action. The student and principal sign the agreement; the student, the parents, and appropriate teachers receive copies. The principal keeps the original. If the agreement is broken, the principal takes the action necessary to administer the most appropriate consequence.

With this approach, students learn that if, for example, they are suspended it is a result of their own actions and not the principal's. If the agreement is kept for an extended period of time, not to exceed a semester except following violent behavior, the student is allowed to tear up the agreement. See an example of a principal-prepared BIA in Figure 4–4. Blank teacher and principal BIAs are located in Appendix C.

FIGURE 4–4
Principal-Prepared Model BIA

BEHAVIOR IMPROVEMENT AGREEMENT
PRINCIPAL

Robert D.   Mr. J
_____   _____
Student   Homeroom Teacher

0054321   Mrs. L.
_____   _____
ID. #   Recommending Teacher

6th   12-5-97
_____   _____
Grade/Class   Date

PROMISED BEHAVIORS

I, ____Robert D_____, . **agree** and **promise** to do the following:

1.) To refrain from any form of disrespect to any teacher or adult
in the building

2.) To avoid any form of aggressive behavior including hitting or striking
while at school or school-sponsored events

3.) To write a letter of apology to Mrs. L. within 48 hours

Failure to keep this agreement will result in the issuance of the following
consequences:

CONSEQUENCES

A.) School suspension (1–3 days)

B.) Required parent conference prior to readmission to classes

C.) Legal action

SIGNATURES

Robert D.   Dr. R
_____   _____
Student   Principal

Q: What happens when dangerous or unacceptable behavior occurs elsewhere in the school?

A: The faculty must decide how to handle serious student misbehavior outside the classroom. One suggestion is that any student discovered in serious conflict on the grounds, in hallways, on buses, or anywhere in the building be escorted by a faculty member to the ICU. Intensive care can be used as a major consequence when a member of the student patrol gives a directive to a student who is not following school standards and the student refuses to comply or becomes hostile. Student patrols should notify the nearest staff member available. That adult then directs the child to go to the ICU. Just as in the classroom, if a student fails to go to the ICU when directed, the office is informed by the most appropriate means available, and a member of the administrative team removes the child using appropriate and effective means. The principal may elect to leave the student in intensive care and speak to the student later about the problem. The principal may also use a BIA or take more serious action.

DESIGNING A SCHOOLWIDE DISCIPLINE PLAN

To better design the discipline plan for schoolwide use, a review team is formed. Or, a school improvement committee already in existence can serve as the review team.

In the RCM plan, the review team is called the DRC. This team should be composed of parents, administrators, students, and teachers. The team should have no more than eight members. After electing a chairperson, the team designs the plan for the school. Note: A DRC is required at the middle school, junior high, and high school levels. It is optional in the elementary school. Many schools hire a full-time ICU coordinator to supervise the unit, but support people are still needed. The ICU should always have two support people: one to remain for supervision and one to get students from the classroom when called.

The school plan is developed by the DRC and should contain the overall school standards and school guidelines as recommended by the faculty and student representatives. After each set of guidelines, such as guidelines for behavior in the hall, parking lot, cafeteria, and so on, a *specific* consequence is described. Procedures for staff to follow in working with infractions by students should be included. The DRC presents the school plan to the administration, faculty, and staff for adoption or modification.

Next, individual teachers or teams establish classroom guidelines (based on school standards) and establish a pool of logical consequences to be used within the classroom. We recommend that students have input into the process of formulating these guidelines. This allows students to be more involved in decision making, and it models participatory citizenship. The teachers develop consequences. These consequences are not posted. Plans are submitted to the DRC for review.

Once the classroom plans are added to the school plan, the administration and staff must establish an ICU. Space is prepared, and a supervisory schedule is developed. As mentioned, two persons should be assigned to the ICU at all times. For example, two staff members can be assigned to

The DRC (Discipline Review Committee) guides and provides assistance to staff in the final steps of developing the RCM plan.

the ICU full-time, teachers can rotate and serve as monitors, or administrators can assist with monitoring.

The DRC monitors how effectively the ICU is used by teachers. The team also assists teachers who need more guidance in ICU procedures and reports to the principal intentional abuse of the ICU by any teacher.

Students are notified of school procedures by teachers at the grade level, by the principal, or by a highly respected staff member. The final stage is notification of parents of the plan by letter and at Open House, both preferably before school begins.

It would be ideal to have an effective, responsibility-oriented classroom management plan such as RCM available for disruptive students but used infrequently. One goal of every master teacher should be to have a problem-free instructional climate in which every child feels successful and, therefore, has no incentive to act inappropriately.

Once school standards, guidelines, and consequences are determined, the team writes a plan for working with extremely difficult students.

Steps for Working with Difficult Students and the Discipline Review Committee

    1. The student breaks a standard or guideline. A consequence is given.

       Type A Behavior   Legal/Antisocial—The student is taken to the principal.

Type B Behavior   Inappropriate behaviors—The student is
                       assigned to the ICU.

2. ICU Procedures
   First Offense   ICU personnel call the parent.
   Second Offense   A parent conference is conducted with the
                        principal and the teachers who sent the
                        student to the ICU on each occasion.
   Third Offense   The ICU coordinator or supervisor con-
                        tacts the individuals who placed the stu-
                        dent in the ICU each of the three times.
                        These individuals write the BIA and sub-
                        mit it to the DRC for approval. Copies are
                        forwarded to all teachers of the student
                        who are involved in the BIA, the student,
                        his or her parents, and the principal.

3. BIA students do not return to the ICU after the third offense for
   any reason. They meet weekly or monthly with the DRC, a faculty mentor, or a student mentor. The DRC can modify or void
   the contract at any time.

4. If the BIA is broken, the student is sent to the principal by a
   member of the DRC, the teacher, or the adult who witnessed the
   infraction of the BIA.

5. A member of the DRC, the witness to the infraction, and the
   principal determine the next action. The DRC is informed in
   writing of the results. These results are filed where all certified
   staff may review them.

6. If the student is placed on an administrative BIA, an administrator meets with the student on a predetermined basis. If improvement is noticed, the principal may refer the student back to the
   DRC for reconsideration.

7. If the administrative BIA is broken, the student is suspended
   immediately, based on state law and local board policy.

8. When the student returns to school, the student is placed on a
   reduced schedule (as determined by the administrative team) and
   assigned to a daily group/individual counseling session with a
   trained counselor. The counselor informs the administration of
   the student's progress. The counselor can recommend outside
   assistance that is within the laws of the state.

9. If the student's behavior does not improve in counseling, the
   DRC, counselor, central office personnel, legal advisor, and
   administrative team representative meet to recommend the
   next step. This may include such options as alternative
   classes, evening school, alternative school, juvenile court, or
   expulsion.

CLASSROOM SITUATIONS

Why are some students "perfect monsters" for one teacher but, while not perfect, at least civil and responsive to another? Through thoughtfully designed classroom management strategies, teachers can encourage responsible behavior by students. Teachers must know at all times what they expect the students to do. The students must know at all times what they are expected to do.

What procedures can be established to assist students in beginning the day on a positive note? What is the routine of student activity on arrival in the classroom before the start of the instructional day? Teachers need a few minutes to reflect on morning routines. Expectations for the following activities need to be developed: storage of outdoor clothing; return of homework assignments; location for returning notes (excuses for absence, transportation changes, work signed by parents, permission forms); trips to the school store, rest room, office, and cafeteria; morning work assignments; and sharpening pencils. After class discussions and role playing, teachers can post checklists in classrooms to remind students of expectations and their related responsibilities. Expectations need to be reviewed, and students need to engage in additional role playing during the year before needs arise.

What are some of the activities in which students engage during instruction that not only can take their attention from schoolwork but also can distract other students and the teacher? Procedures must be established for these activities to structure the day and to provide increased opportunity for maximum engagement in learning. Written guidelines addressing these activities need to be clarified for students. For older students, teachers can brainstorm a list of distractions, develop preventive procedures, and discuss natural and logical consequences during a class meeting. Activities that might be identified include use of the pencil sharpener, individual trips to the rest room, discarding trash, illness during instruction, spontaneous thoughts students want to share with the teacher, or a need for tissue or paper.

Homework: A Major Problem

How should homework be assigned? What can be done to increase the odds of students' taking home the needed textbooks, materials, and written descriptions of assignments? Teachers should brainstorm and develop organizational tips for students that will assist them in being prepared for successful completion, safekeeping, and return of homework assignments.

Enlisting student assistance in developing guidelines for homework will result in increased student ownership of responsibility for its completion. We developed the following set of guidelines with input from students:

1. Homework will be planned to require no more than X minutes per night (for example, 40 minutes for fourth grade).
2. Parents can help with homework because it is always practice.
3. Whenever a student cannot understand the work, he or she may try for ten minutes and then quit.
4. If the class is not taught, the homework assignment is canceled.
5. If homework is not completed on time, the student will choose a time to complete it within parameters specified by the teacher.

Disruptive Classroom Behavior

How do the majority of students in the classroom feel about the behaviors of other students that interfere with their right to a safe, orderly, and inviting learning environment? Teachers can plan opportunities to involve students in discussions and role-playing activities that address student reaction to the disruptive behaviors of other students. A consequence for engaging in disruptive behaviors during instruction might be that the student sit at a table or desk at the rear of the classroom during part of the class. A sign-in sheet might be kept at that spot to document that the student's disruptive behavior prevented the student from participating in the usual manner in a class activity.

The preceding procedures define expectations for responsible behavior by students and clearly communicate these expectations, thus eliminating the potential for many problems.

RESPONDING TO STUDENT ACTIONS

Each time teachers interact with a student individually or as a member of a group during the school day, they have an opportunity to influence the behavior of that student. Words and actions determine whether the influence is positive or negative. Emotional tone conveys to students whether or not they are worthy of respect and able to succeed. Teachers must affirm students' ability to act responsibly by establishing an expectation that they will act responsibly. That expectation must be reinforced through consistent teacher response to unacceptable behavior through the enforcement of natural or logical consequences.

Following are scenarios of situations that occur in every classroom. Samples of inappropriate and appropriate teacher reactions to each situation are included.

Elementary School Scenarios

Scenario 1

Kelly is a loner. She has been ostracized by other students because of her difficulty in approaching other children to become friends. Jennifer is asked to be Kelly's partner for a class activity. She responds emphatically, "No! If I touch Kelly, I'll get bad germs!"

Inappropriate Response

"Jennifer, that's ridiculous. You won't get anything by being Kelly's partner! Since you responded that way, you just sit next to Kelly and hold her hand while you work together." (Jennifer is seen later in the day with one sleeve rolled up and one sleeve down. Why? Fear of contamination.)

Acceptable Response

"Jennifer, that was very rude." "Kelly, I would like for you to be my partner for this activity." It's not the words that make a difference in this instance. It is the teacher's gentle grasp of Kelly's hand and light touch on her chin that soften the blow and demonstrate to other students that Jennifer's fear is unfounded. When it is too late to avoid hurt feelings, the teacher's response can model kindness and acceptance.

RCM Response

Be proactive. How much thought was given to the request that Jennifer be Kelly's partner for this activity? Are there other children in this classroom who may have responded in a more positive manner? However, because the action has already occurred, Jennifer is limited to working by herself, and the teacher carefully selects another partner for Kelly.

Scenario 2

It's time for art.

Inappropriate Response

"Students, line up to go to art class." Mass chaos follows as everyone dashes into line. A shoving match occurs after one child breaks into line in front of another. This results in two children getting their names on the board. "Every day someone has problems lining up! Why can't you children act like human beings?"

Acceptable Response

"John, you are our line leader today. OK, door holder, please line up next. John, call students to line up by tables to go to art." Children line up in a quiet and orderly fashion with no discord. "Folks, you must be the best class in this school. Thank you."

RCM Response

The teacher asks for class attention, pauses, and visually surveys to demonstrate her expectation that students will follow her directive. She then quietly states, "Line up for art, please. Thank you." No more is necessary, because procedures for lining up to leave the classroom were taught effectively at the beginning of the year, reviewed and practiced periodically, and acknowledged routinely. Class helpers are assigned at the beginning of each week.

Nothing is more distressful for some students than to be door holder and lose their place near the front of the line or to be the person the door holder slips in front of in line after holding the door. At the beginning of the year, establish the expectation that children will take turns being door holder. Establish the procedure that the door holder will always go to the end of the line.

Scenario 3

Charles has not turned in his homework.

Inappropriate Response

The teacher addresses Charles at his desk from her desk. "Charles, where is your homework? Why don't you have it? You left it at home? Charles, at least twice a week, we go through this routine. Aren't you getting as tired of it as I am? Well, that's another zero. If it doesn't bother you, it doesn't bother me."

Acceptable Response

"Charles, please turn in your homework. You don't have it? Come to my desk, please." Softly, "Charles, it is your responsibility to complete your assignments. You have a choice. You may complete your homework during the day after your class assignments have been done or remain after school to complete it."

RCM Response

As part of the early morning routine, this teacher scans the homework assignments of students who have developed a habit of not doing homework, turning it in incomplete, or having excessive errors. Depending on the needs of the individual student, the teacher routinely provides modified homework assignments or directs the student to complete or correct the written assignment before breakfast, rest room visits, trips to the school store, and socializing with classmates.

Middle School Scenarios

Scenario 1

Christy and Lynn are carrying on a whispered conversation during a social studies lecture. It's not the first time.

Inappropriate Response

"Christy, Lynn, pay attention, please. Girls, I'll tell you one more time. Stop talking. Girls, every time you sit together you talk. Stop talking now and pay attention." The talking continues. It's ignored.

Acceptable Response

The teacher is waiting at the door when Christy and Lynn enter the classroom. A quiet conversation follows.

"Girls, it has become obvious that when you sit together, you visit, regardless of what you should be doing. I think that it's great that you enjoy each other's company so much. However, it's not OK for you to carry on your conversations during class. I am assigning you seats on opposite sides of the room. When we are not actively involved in instruction and your work has been completed in a satisfactory manner, you may visit."

"Mrs. Hunt, that's not fair!"

"When you are not actively involved in instruction and your work has been completed in a satisfactory manner, you may visit. Christy, sit here, please. Lynn, over here."

RCM Response

As students work on an independent assignment, Mrs. Hunt calls the two girls to the door. She positions herself at the door to speak privately to the girls as she surveys the working students. "Girls, it's important that you have the opportunity to learn as much as you can in this class. When you sit near each other, you do not give adequate attention to your work. You talk too much. Here are your new seating assignments, effective tomorrow. When your attention to instruction improves, I will give you an opportunity to return to your original seats."

Scenario 2

Students are returning to the classroom from the media center, "Mr. Cline, Mr. Cline, Derek hit me on the head with his library book."

Inappropriate Response

Mr. Cline stops the line in the hallway and walks back to Derek, finger pointing. "Derek James, how many times have I told you to keep your hands to yourself? Don't you get tired of hearing me fuss at you? When are you going to start doing what you're suppose to do? Give me that book. When we get back to the classroom, start writing 100 times, 'I must keep my hands, feet, and objects to myself.' You will finish it for science homework."

Acceptable Response

"Derek, walk with me, please." On return to the classroom, Mr. Cline instructs the class to put away their library books and get out last night's math homework to review with a partner. (Early in the year, Mr. Cline established a procedure for peer homework check to precede group review.) He then speaks individually to Derek. "Derek, this is the third time this week—and it's Wednesday—that I've had reports of your difficulty in maintaining self-control as we move through the building. For the remainder of the week, your place in line will be next to me. Next week you may return to the group. However, at the first report that you are bothering others, your place will again be next to me. You are responsible for controlling your behavior in line." Soft grumbling and mumbling follow this directive. It's ignored. Derek "forgets" to walk next to Mr. Cline for the next trip out of the classroom. Mr. Cline matter-of-factly directs Derek to walk next to him. Derek takes his time getting there. Mr. Cline calmly waits. It is necessary for Mr. Cline to repeat this exercise with Derek at least three times before Derek realizes that Mr. Cline means what he says. However, Mr. Cline's patience and consistency do result in an improvement in Derek's attitude and behavior.

RCM Response

Mr. Cline has observed on previous occasions when students have "told on" Derek for bothering them that Derek has never shown malicious intent in the attention he directs to his classmates. He appears to want to establish a friendship, but he just does not have the social skills to approach other students appropriately. Mr. Cline discusses with Derek how he might become noticed by someone with whom he would like to be friends in a way that does not appear threatening to that student. He also asks the school counselor to involve his class in guidance activities that will assist Derek and other students with similar needs to approach other students differently. These activities also help other students in the class recognize the difference between positive and negative attention by their peers more effectively.

Scenario 3

Sean calls out answers to many questions during the discussion of the story the class just read. This is not an isolated incident. Sean is a bright child. His responses are on target. However, his interjections discourage many other students from volunteering to share responses.

Inappropriate Response

Ms. Staley acknowledges Sean's responses, sometimes asking additional questions to encourage further detail. She then reminds him to raise his hand and wait to be identified before he responds to future questions. The scene is repeated.

Acceptable Response

Ms. Staley conferences privately with Sean and informs him that his continual call-outs are unacceptable. Although she wants him to be part of the discussion, she informs him that after his first call-out he will be removed to time-out and not be allowed to participate in the discussion.

RCM Response 1

As Sean begins his call-out response, Ms. Staley looks at him, states his name, and raises her hand to remind Sean of what he is expected to do if he has something to contribute. She then calls on another child to answer. This action is repeated each time that Sean calls out. She sometimes identifies Sean in advance when a question is for him. Sean eventually recognizes that his responses will not be acknowledged under his terms and begins to raise his hand. Although Ms. Staley does not call on him every time he does so, she tacitly affirms his compliance with procedures and privately recognizes his efforts to refrain from calling out.

RCM Response 2

Ms. Staley established a routine early in the year of providing wait-time before identifying someone to answer her questions. This holds all students accountable for forming mental responses. Students have role played this in games. Sean's impulsiveness was identified then. Ms. Staley recognized that this procedure did not stop Sean's call-outs. She also noted other impulsive behaviors. Therefore, she brought her concerns about Sean's behavior to the attention of his parents and learning assistance team. Appropriate individualized strategies were created and implemented after discussion and observation indicated that Sean had attention deficit hyperactivity disorder.

Secondary School Scenarios

Scenario 1

The students are taking an English test. Pencil tapping starts near the back of the room. Students look up from their work to identify the source of the noise. It's Tony.

Inappropriate Response

Mrs. Walker walks back to Tony's desk. "Tony, get back to work. Tony, that pencil tapping is distracting to the other students. Stop it. Tony, if you don't stop tapping, I'll take away the pencil and you won't be able to finish the test. (That suits Tony.) Tony . . . . "

Acceptable Response

Mrs. Walker walks back to Tony's desk and lightly but firmly places her hand on Tony's hand; the tapping stops. She removes her hand; the tapping resumes. Mrs. Walker quietly states, "Tony, stop tapping the pencil, and complete the test now." The tapping continues. Mrs. Walker removes the pencil and test paper from Tony's desk. She tells him that arrangements will be made for him to complete the test after lunch.

RCM Response 1

Mrs. Walker learns from conversations with Tony's previous teacher and his parents that Tony unconsciously makes noises with objects in his hand as he concentrates on tasks. She observes other students as they work to see if Tony's actions disturb them as much as they disturb her. Other students appear unconcerned. Mrs. Walker ignores the tapping this time and plans to find a small sponge ball for the end of Tony's pencil so future tapping will not be distracting to her.

RCM Response 2

It is obvious to Mrs. Walker that Tony is tapping his pencil to be disruptive. It is affecting the efforts of other students to concentrate on the test. Mrs. Walker sends Tony to the ICU and makes arrangements for him to complete the test after school. Mrs. Walker had communicated to parents early in the school year her use of "after-school detention" as a consequence for some inappropriate behaviors. The majority of parents, including Tony's, supported her use of this strategy. Parents agreed to provide transportation home. In some instances, Mrs. Walker arranges for students to be in detention before school if this eases transportation problems for parents.

Scenario 2

Barbara gets out of her seat during a class discussion and begins roaming around the room.

Inappropriate Response

Mrs. Scott notices that Barbara is wandering.

"Barbara, what are you doing?"

"I need a pencil."

"Barbara, you don't need a pencil right now. Return to your seat."

"But I need a pencil."

"Return to your seat now or I'll call the office."

"What did I do wrong?"

No matter what Mrs. Scott does now, Barbara has won, and Mrs. Scott has lost. It will take several minutes to fully focus the rest of the class on instruction.

RCM Acceptable Response (Reactive)

"Barbara, return to your seat."

"But I need a pencil."

"Barbara, return to your seat."

"But. . . . "

Mrs. Scott calmly arranges for Barbara to go to the ICU.

RCM Response (Proactive)

Mrs. Scott has observed that during class discussions Barbara has a tendency to get restless. She is not an auditory learner. She is easily distracted when she is not actively involved in instruction. Therefore, Mrs. Scott circulates during class discussions. She positions herself near Barbara's desk and occasionally refocuses Barbara's attention on the discussion by directing a question to her or lightly resting her hand on her shoulder. She has also found that Barbara is a doodler. Her doodling does not appear to interfere with her ability to listen. It does help keep her in her seat.

Scenario 3

Blows are exchanged in the boys' rest room during lunch period.

Inappropriate Response

The boys are taken to the principal, who sends them home for the day (reward) or paddles both boys (punishes violence with violence).

Acceptable Response

The two students are escorted to their homeroom teachers by the staff member who broke up the fight. The teachers call the parents of both boys and hold a conference. These students are directed to stay away from each other until a student mediation hearing can be scheduled.

RCM Response

The two students are taken to the ICU by the staff member who broke up the fight. During investigation of the incident, the teacher learns that one student had been bullying the other, who finally had taken all he could take. The bully loses the privilege of moving through the school without adult supervision during lunch period. Arrangements are made with the school counselor for counseling. The other student is counseled by the teacher on acceptable responses to bullying by other students (specifically, to avoid situations in which the possibility of such an outcome might result and to inform a staff member when being victimized by a bully).

As the scenarios demonstrate, the teacher's words, tone of voice, facial expression, and body movement can be used subtly yet effectively to deliver expectations to students in a discrete, nonembarrassing manner. In each instance, the teacher's knowledge about the individual child influenced the teacher's reaction to the behavior. All incidents of inappropriate student behavior cannot be resolved easily. However, teachers can limit the number of classroom disruptions through demonstrating the expectation that when student behavior is identified as unacceptable, teachers will effectively address it in a manner that is fair to that individual child. Sometimes disruptive behaviors cannot be satisfactorily addressed without causing increased disruption of instruction. Teachers' professional judgment and previous experience with individual students can be used to make decisions about when the ICU or behavior contracts are appropriate.

We all have our bad days. Shouldn't we acknowledge that our students have bad days, too? We are mature adults. Our students are maturing children. They may not handle their bad days as well as we do. Our problems may appear big. Does that make their problems less significant?

PUTTING CONCEPTS INTO PRACTICE

Questions for Discussion and Related Activities

1. How would you handle the following discipline problems? Try to think of several consequences that might be used before using the ICU. Remember to avoid a formula. Each child and each situation are different.

   a. Refusing to do homework

   b. Coming to school late (if it is within the control of the student)

   c. Leaving class without permission

   d. Stealing from a staff member or another student

   e. Name calling, bullying, fighting

   f. Graffiti or property damage

2. Intensive Care Usage: In your group, brainstorm about three other situations for which the ICU may be the first consequence.

3. Consequences Check: Respond individually to the following consequences suggested for the stated problems. After completion, break into groups and compare opinions.

Consequences for General Behavior Problems

   a. Organize a "Citizenship Club." Make membership requirements difficult.

   b. Instead of accusing or confronting the child for breaking a guideline, simply ask, "Are you being responsible?"

   c. Use index card contracts for any repetitive negative behavior. The child signs the agreement. Place the contract on the child's desk for daily referral.

   d. Post a sign on the board entitled "Prevention." At the beginning of the day, ask students, "Who is not going to be responsible today?" If any children raise their hands, ask them to put their name on the sign. Take the students out into the hall individually and see if they are serious. If they were joking, inform the students that this is not responsible behavior and return them to class. If this is repeated, or the students state that they were serious, send them to the ICU immediately. Students who would do this intentionally need to be further evaluated for a problem such as emotional imbalance.

   e. Use reminders. These are just simple statements to help students get back on task. These are not threats or warnings.

   f. Limit a student's activity. This is better used with directives than with guidelines. If a student does not follow a directive, limit the child's participation in the activity.

   g. Request administrative input. The principal can address each grade level or class on a weekly basis to show support for the discipline program. This can be done on morning or afternoon visits to the class during noninstructional time. Also, the principal should address expectations of responsible behavior in daily announcements.

   h. Notify parents of the school's behavior management plan, and periodically inform parents of their child's adherence to the plan. Send letters home when the plan is first implemented and annually thereafter, informing the parents of the school's discipline plan. Get the parents' and students' signature on a copy of the plan that is returned to the school. The back of this notification can be used to record consequences for the student.

Consequences for Problems with Homework

a. Use homework for practice of a learned skill only.

b. Use homework for preparation for new learning only.

c. Don't assign any. Evaluate how big a problem homework really is. If it's a major problem, have students do it in class.

d. Arrange for students who do not complete their homework to do it during lunch, during free time, or after school.

e. Individualize homework according to ability.

f. Give a homework period during the school day.

g. Make homework interactive instead of drill. Let students have input into the selection of homework projects—written, model, oral presentation, and so on.

h. Allow students to keep homework in a folder. Make it self-checking with records.

i. Arrange a procedure so that parents check off and sign homework daily.

j. Arrange for students who did not do their homework to complete it while other children do the present class activity. Those students have to make up the class activity during free time.

Consequences for Students Who Are Not Prepared for Class

a. The students are not permitted to participate in the activity. They do an alternative activity or sit out because they are not prepared for class.

b. The children do the missed activity during a free period or after school.

c. The children rent paper or pencil from the teacher and must pay the teacher a rental fee (preferably through service to the teacher such as cleaning the board).

d. Design a cooperative contract with the parent for related consequences at home.

e. Organize an "I Am Prepared to Learn" club. Provide certificates of membership for students who are routinely prepared for class.

f. Contact parents and schedule a conference for students who are not prepared for class more than twice in any week. Watch for habits forming.

Consequences for Students Who Refuse to Do Any Work

a. These students cannot participate in any group activity.

b. Have parent conferences and/or inform parents through a check sheet—daily, if necessary.

c. Use the Freeze Technique (three to six weeks). See Figure 4–2.

Consequences Involving Group Assistance for General Behavior Problems

a. Establish grade-level teacher advisory groups with participation by administrative staff as a viable option. In this setting, create specific plans for improvement for any student who is not acting responsibly. For example, this group could write the BIA for a student.

b. If a student's behavior continues to disrupt the class, schedule a hearing with a Class Court of peers. Just as in court, the student is charged by another student with an inappropriate act. The accused student is brought to court and admits guilt or offers a defense for a plea of not guilty. The case is heard in the teacher's presence. The court serves as judge and jury and recommends any consequence for a finding of guilty to the teacher. The teacher uses professional judgment in assigning or modifying the proposed consequence. This is best used for grades three and up. Choose six of the most responsible students to be the court. Change membership as necessary.

Consequences for Antisocial Behaviors

A student should be immediately removed from the class and taken to the principal for any of the following activities:

a. Fighting
b. Drugs/alcohol
c. Verbal/physical threats
d. Vandalism/major stealing
e. Weapons

Do not attempt to use the RCM plan for any of these behaviors.

Words of Caution

The RCM plan serves two major purposes. The plan's goal is to teach students to value and practice responsible behavior. The second purpose is to use RCM as a classroom management tool to address disruptive behaviors by use of logical consequences that allow students to self-correct their behavior. A cautionary note to educators using the plan: Avoid formulas for addressing specific behaviors. Every student and every situation is different. RCM will work if implemented as designed. However, patterns of teacher behavior with responses to student actions that treat all students the same can and will sabotage a teacher's best intentions.

It is your actions—not your words—that teach responsibility.

A Cautionary Tale

A school used the RCM Plan. Things went well until a few teachers used the ICU as a dumping ground for all disruptive behaviors; hence, these teachers were not responsible teachers. The patterns of behavior of these teachers were so predictable that the secretaries placed bets as to time of day, type of disruption, and specific staff member who would call for the ICU. This continued until the ICU for these teachers became totally ineffective. Soon the ICU was removed and the RCM plan discarded to allow teachers to return to bribery, punishment, external control, and equal treatment of all students.

Some teachers may be concerned that a dramatic change in disciplinary procedures will be too difficult an adjustment for students. If the procedures that we have discussed are followed completely, there will be no problem in transition.

Responsible
Classroom
Management Models

As stated throughout this text, the RCM plan can be used at the elementary, middle, and high school levels at the schoolwide, team, or individual classroom levels. The most effective model of the plan is the schoolwide model. In this chapter, we describe specific procedures for implementing RCM in elementary, middle, and high schools and describe models for each. We also detail RCM transition and team models.

THE ELEMENTARY SCHOOL PLAN

Faculty members present the school plan to the Discipline Review Committee (DRC) for review. Once the DRC reviews the plan, it presents it to the full faculty for consensus.

Steps for Implementation

In implementing the schoolwide elementary model, the following steps should be used:

Step 1. Review how the RCM plan differs from other classroom management models (see Chapter 1).

Major Focus: Using the RCM plan, educators teach students how to be responsible and allow students to self-correct inappropriate behavior.

Step 2. Review the major aspects of growth and development, focusing primarily on the elementary school years (see Chapter 2).

Major Focus: Children go through various stages of growth and development. Review how these different stages of development impact learning and classroom behavior.

Step 3. Review the major principles of the RCM plan, and analyze the major research findings of the pilot and model RCM schools (see Chapter 3).

Major Focus: RCM is research-based and has a high degree of success when the principles of the model are followed completely.

Step 4. Design a warm and inviting school for all students (see Chapter 3).

Major Focus: An inviting environment is conducive to higher motivation and learning. It helps build a sense of community.

Step 5. Establish the school standard(s) (see Chapter 4).

Major Focus: Either the full faculty or an elected DRC determines the school standard(s). Input from parents and students is strongly encouraged. We recommend the use of one school standard initially.

146

Interact with students and get to know them.

The most effective standard has been "I am responsible for all my actions."

Step 6. Establish school guidelines that are to be monitored by the entire faculty and staff.

Major Focus: School guidelines focus more on behavior outside the classroom, especially in hall, lunchroom, and playground situations. However, these can focus on behaviors such as disrespect or vulgarity in the classroom. In this case, a school guideline (such as respect) is automatically part of the classroom plan. A school guideline can be used as the first classroom guideline.

Step 7. Develop one specific consequence for each school guideline (see Chapter 4).

Major Focus: The process of developing specific consequences will keep all of the faculty and staff focused on a schoolwide model. Every adult should work in harmony—no territorial protection. For example, if a first-grade teacher sees a violation of a school guideline by a fourth grader, she enforces the consequences.

Step 8. Each teacher or grade level develops guidelines for individual classrooms (see Chapter 4).

Major Focus: Teachers work in a democratic process with students to determine specific guidelines. When the program is first being used by a school and later in lower grades, teachers will provide more structure and direct suggestions for the process. These guidelines are posted in the classroom underneath the school standard(s).

Step 9.   Create a collection of logical consequences for classroom or team-level use (see Chapter 4).

Major Focus: Classroom consequences are not posted; instead, the teacher has numerous consequences that can be individualized for maximum effectiveness.

Step 10.   Develop a classroom instructional plan that introduces the concept of responsibility as RCM is implemented. Responsibility, character development, and civility should be integrated in appropriate instructional situations throughout the year (see Chapter 4).

Major Focus: The more responsibility is taught and expected, the greater the effectiveness of the plan.

Step 11.   Establish a schoolwide Intensive Care Unit (ICU) with a schedule, personnel, and procedures (see Chapter 4).

Major Focus: The ICU is used schoolwide for behaviors that require ICU placement and for major classroom disruptions.

Step 12.   Determine when and how Behavior Improvement Agreements (BIAs) will be used (see Chapter 4).

Major Focus: BIAs are used after ICU has been ineffective. The classroom teacher should write the BIA. If the BIA is broken, the principal can design a BIA.

Step 13.   Develop procedures for informing parents of the RCM plan.

Major Focus: Parents need to be informed and encouraged to participate. We suggest that the parent package include the following:
1. Letter from the principal
2. Open House or Parent Meeting to answer questions
3. Copy of the school standard, guidelines, and consequences
4. Letter from the teacher listing and explaining the classroom or grade-level guidelines and procedures
5. Explanations of logical consequences, ICU, and BIA, which are provided by the DRC and/or Administrative Team (usually made up of the principal and assistant principal)
6. Form for parents and students to sign indicating that they understand the program

Step 14.   Develop procedures for informing students in the elementary school.

Major Focus: Students should be involved in the process, but at this level, teachers will have to be more directive initially. We suggest that the student package include the following:

1. Principal's introduction of the RCM plan to students by grade level in the gym or multipurpose room
2. Teacher's introduction to students of the school standard(s), school guidelines, and grade-level or classroom guidelines
3. Discussion of logical consequences, ICU, and BIA

Step 15.   Decide if a transitional approach would be more effective in the school during the first year of using the RCM plan (see the schoolwide transition model later in this chapter).

Major Focus: The transitional plan can be used at the beginning of the year to ease from a more external model or at any time after the beginning of the year when the RCM plan is first implemented.

Exemplary Elementary School Model

This section shows an exemplary elementary school RCM model that can be used as written or modified to meet individual school needs. The model includes the school standard and guidelines, consequences for classroom use, ICU and BIA procedures, and procedures for introducing RCM to parents, students, and teachers.

School Standard

I am responsible for my actions at all times.

School Guidelines

Guideline 1	Any serious or continuous act of student behavior that disrupts the educational process will not be tolerated.
Consequence	The observing adult will take the student to the ICU, and the homeroom teacher will be informed by the ICU supervisor.
Guideline 2	Using profanity or obscene language is not allowed.
Consequence	The observing adult will take the student to the ICU, and the homeroom teacher will be informed by the ICU supervisor.
Guideline 3	Failure to respond to a reasonable request by an adult, or lying or cheating to deceive school authorities will not be tolerated.
Consequence	The observing adult will take the student to the ICU, and the homeroom teacher will be informed by the ICU supervisor.

Guideline 4   Illegal or antisocial behaviors will not be tolerated. Examples of these follow:

- Physically attacking or threatening to strike any school employee or any adult at school
- Assaulting, attacking, or threatening to cause physical injury to a student by two or more students, and/or any assault resulting in serious personal injury by one or more students
- Extorting or maliciously threatening another student to gain money or objects belonging to others
- Carrying weapons
- Arson, vandalism, unlawful entry, or theft
- Selling, possessing, distributing, or being under the influence of alcohol, tobacco products, or other drugs
- Verbal threats, physical assaults, or intentional acts that create a clear threat to the safety of others
- Any act of a sexual nature
- Directing obscene language and/or gestures toward any persons
- Leaving class without teacher/principal permission
- Breaking federal, state, or local laws
- Violations of any school district behavior guideline

Consequence   The observing adult immediately notifies the principal to determine legal or other appropriate action.

Guideline 5   Any other violations that are expressly listed in the school or county elementary guidelines or other behaviors or activities that the principal considers inappropriate will not be tolerated.

Consequence   The observing adult will take the student to the principal.

Consequences for Classroom Use

The following consequences can be used at three different levels.

Level 1: No Record Keeping Is Required

- Verbal reminders, for example, "Was that a responsible act?"
- A brief conference with the student immediately after the offense occurs; end the conference with a question such as, "Can I count on you to improve?"

Level 2: Record Keeping Should Be Required

- Limitation—Examples include walking with the teacher in line, isolation, and working in a separate area in the classroom.

Learning can be fun when students know the difference between obedient and responsible behavior.

- Siberia box—Remove disruptive items, and store them until they are returned to the student's parents.
- Time-out—Students sign in to time-out.
- Time-out in another classroom.
- Class meeting.
- Parent/home contact—To inform parents of their child's behavior and the consequences, not necessarily to call them in for a conference.
- Interventions—For example, by a social worker, guidance counselor, nurse, or the Student Services Management Team.

Level 3: Record Keeping Is Required

- ICU for severe behaviors
- BIA, teacher or principal model

The ICU should never be the first consequence. Students should be allowed to progress through level-1 and level-2 consequences before they are sent to the ICU; if not, the program will not be effective with students or parents.

Procedures for the ICU

Step 1. The teacher calls the ICU and identifies the classroom and room number. The teacher says nothing else—only the ICU staff member responds.

Step 2. The ICU staff member escorts the student from the classroom to the ICU.

Step 3. The student is registered for the ICU, using the ICU referral form (which completes the initial paperwork), and is given a seat. No talking is allowed in the ICU.

Step 4.   Within twenty minutes after the child has been escorted from the class, the teacher will go to the ICU and hold a conference with the student.

Step 5.   When the teacher is ready to confer with the student, the teacher will call the ICU and state, "This is (teacher's name) in room (teacher's room number). I am ready to confer with my student in the ICU. I need assistance (or, I do not need assistance)."

Step 6.   The teacher and the student sign an Individual Student Report after a brief conference. The conference will occur in the ICU if that room is unoccupied or (another specified space) if other students are present in the ICU. The student is then escorted back to the classroom.

Step 7.   After the student's first visit to the ICU, the ICU supervisor sends the Individual Student Report to the classroom teacher, principal, and parent. After a student's second visit to the ICU, the ICU supervisor again sends the Individual Student Report to the classroom teacher, principal, and parent. The classroom teacher will also call the parents to inform them of the student's second visit. The classroom teacher can also use this as an opportunity to inform the parents that a BIA will follow if the student has a third visit to the ICU. After the third visit, the ICU supervisor again sends the Individual Student Report to the classroom teacher, principal, and parents. The classroom teacher then prepares a BIA as time allows (see the following BIA procedures).

BIA Procedures

Step 1.   The teacher selects a time to write a BIA with the student in a private setting. When writing promised behaviors, the teacher obtains as much student input as possible. The teacher always assigns the consequence. Two main consequences are (1) report to the principal and/or (2) a parent conference, which is required before the child can return to school. If the teacher needs classroom assistance while writing the BIA with the student, the teacher requests that another staff member or colleague supervise the class.

Step 2.   The teacher gives a copy of the BIA to the student and the principal, mails the original to the parents, and retains one copy. The names of students on BIAs are posted in an assigned place out of public view but accessible to staff. Please note: If the student refuses to sign the BIA, the teacher states that this is a teacher-assigned document, deletes the word *Agreement,* and writes in the word *Assignment.* Then the document does not require the student's signature.

Step 3.   If the BIA is broken, implement one of the stated consequences. No positive consequences are stated on the BIA.

Implementing RCM with Parents, Students, and Teachers

This section describes materials that are useful for introducing RCM to parents, students, and teachers.

1. Parent Package
   a. Principal's cover letter—an introduction to RCM (see Figure 5–1)
   b. School standard(s) and school guidelines with consequences
   c. County elementary education behavior guidelines
   d. Classroom guidelines and specialist guidelines with a parent signature slip (see Figures 5-2 and 5-3)
2. Student Package
   a. School standard(s) and guidelines with consequences
   b. Classroom student guidelines (poster or display)
   c. A unit of instruction on the topic of responsibility

FIGURE 5–1
Elementary Parent/Student Plan Information Letter from the Principal

Dear Parents,

To provide a safe and positive environment for learning, Smith Elementary School has implemented a Responsible Classroom Management (RCM) plan for teachers and students. The RCM plan is based on our educational viewpoint that all children can succeed in school. We believe that all children can be taught responsibility. Reinforcing this belief, the RCM plan requires responsible teachers and staff to deliver quality instruction in an interactive learning environment that is safe, clean, and inviting.

The school standard at Smith is "I am responsible for my actions at all times." It is our responsibility as educators, as it is your responsibility as parents, to teach and expect students to practice responsibility.

The RCM plan serves two major purposes. The plan's goal is to teach students to value and practice responsible behavior. The second purpose is to use RCM as a classroom management tool to address disruptive behaviors by the use of logical consequences.

As we quickly approach the next century, employers know the importance of having well-educated and responsible employees. Our goal is to help all students reach their fullest potential. This can be achieved only through quality instruction; effective management of classroom behavior; maintenance of a learning environment that is safe, orderly, and inviting; and the expectation that students be responsible for their actions at all times.

I am looking forward to working with each of you this year.

Sincerely,

(Principal)

FIGURE 5–2
Elementary Parent–Student Plan Information Letter from the Teacher

Dear Parents,

    This year we will be learning in our class that we must be responsible for all our actions at Smith Elementary School. We will be learning that responsibility means doing what is right, that cooperation means working with others, and that respect means caring for others. We will be reading a number of books and talking about how the characters in the story did or did not show responsibility, cooperation, or respect.

    Our classroom guidelines follow:

        To be a responsible student in fourth grade, I will . . .

        Come to class prepared and ready to learn.

        Respect the rights, property, and safety of myself and others.

        Cooperate with my teacher and fellow classmates.

Sincerely,

(Fourth grade Teachers)

- -

Please sign and return bottom portion.

My child and I have read and discussed the classroom guidelines.

_____	_____
Parent's Signature	Student's Signature
_____	_____
Date	Date

       d. Administration's introduction of the RCM plan and the ICU to children by grade levels, meeting in a multipurpose room on the first day of school

  3. Staff Procedures for Implementation of RCM

       a. All staff members who did not attend all sessions of the RCM training are responsible for learning about the program. They should ask their grade level colleagues for information.

       b. Review the classroom guidelines, parent package, and RCM plan with parents during Open House; send home the parent package; send a follow-up package for any student who has not returned the signed slip by the due date. Then note that attempts were made to provide parents with the information.

       c. Place the school standard(s) in hallways, the cafeteria, and the multipurpose room.

       d. Unit of Instruction: Develop a plan in writing describing how you will incorporate responsibility into instruction. It can be an individual or grade-level/group plan.

FIGURE 5–3
Elementary Parent–Student Plan Information Letter from the Specialists, for
Signature and Return

Dear Parents,

    All specialists at Smith Elementary (AG, Art, French, Guidance, Music, PE, Resource, Speech) are also participating in the Responsible Classroom Management plan at our school. We have adopted the following guidelines for special classes:

    To be a responsible student in special classes, each student will . . .

        Come to class prepared to learn.

        Put forth his/her best effort.

        Respect others' rights.

                                Sincerely,

                                (Specialists)

- -

Please sign and return bottom portion.

My child and I have read and discussed the classroom guidelines.

_____   _____
Parent's Signature   Student's Signature

_____   _____
Date   Date

    e. RCM Record Keeping: Use an organized system of recording consequences for violations of school and classroom guidelines.

    f. While hallway, cafeteria, and multipurpose room procedures are still being discussed, submit any suggestions in writing to the appropriate staff member or any member of the DRC.

    g. The administration will determine the ICU supervisor duties and provide them to the staff. School staff ICU duties include (1) supervision of the ICU; (2) relieving classroom teachers when necessary; (3) serving thirty-minute intervals; (4) assisting the ICU supervisor with the initial paperwork when necessary.

THE MIDDLE SCHOOL PLAN

Steps for Implementation

In the middle school schoolwide model, the following steps should be used:

Step 1.   Review how the RCM plan differs from other classroom management models (see Chapter 1).

Major Focus: Using the RCM plan, educators teach students how to be responsible and allow students to self-correct inappropriate behavior.

Step 2.   Review the major aspects of growth and development, focusing primarily on the adolescent years (see Chapter 2).

Major Focus: Children go through various stages of growth and development. Review how these different stages of development impact learning and classroom behavior.

Step 3.   Review the major principles of the RCM plan, and analyze the major research findings of the pilot and model RCM schools (see Chapter 3).

Major Focus: RCM is research-based and has a high degree of success when the principles of the model are followed completely.

Step 4.   Design a warm and inviting school for all students (see Chapter 3).

Major Focus: An inviting environment is conducive to higher motivation and learning. It helps build a sense of community.

Step 5.   Establish the school standard(s) (see Chapter 4).

Major Focus: Either the full faculty or an elected DRC determines the school standard(s). Input from parents and students is strongly encouraged at the middle school level. We recommend that one school standard be used initially. The most effective standard has been "I am responsible for all my actions."

Step 6.   Establish school guidelines that are to be monitored by the entire faculty and staff.

Major Focus: School guidelines focus more on behavior outside of the classroom, especially in the hall, lunchroom, and outdoor situations. However, these can focus on behaviors such as disrespect or vulgarity in the classroom. In this case, a school guideline (such as respect) is automatically part of the classroom plan. A school guideline can be used as the first classroom guideline.

Step 7.   Develop one specific consequence for each school guideline (see Chapter 4).

Major Focus: The process of developing specific consequences will keep all of the faculty and staff focused on a schoolwide model. Every adult should work in harmony—no territorial protection. For example, if a sixth-grade math teacher sees a violation of a school guideline by an eighth grader, she enforces the consequences.

Step 8.   Each teacher or content team develops guidelines for individual classrooms (see Chapter 4).

Major Focus: Teachers work in a democratic process with students to determine specific guidelines. When the program is first implemented, the teacher will provide more structure and direct suggestions for the process. These guidelines are posted in the classroom underneath the school standard(s).

Step 9.   Create a collection of logical consequences for classroom or team-level use (see Chapter 4).

Major Focus: Classroom consequences are not posted; instead, the teacher or team has numerous consequences that can be individualized for maximum effectiveness.

Step 10.   Develop a classroom instructional plan that introduces the concept of responsibility as RCM is implemented. Responsibility, character development, and civility should be integrated in appropriate instructional situations, especially in social studies, throughout the year (see Chapter 4).

Major Focus: The more responsibility is taught and expected, the greater the effectiveness of the plan.

Step 11.   Establish a schoolwide ICU complete with a schedule, personnel, and procedures (see Chapter 4).

Major Focus: The ICU is used schoolwide for behaviors that require ICU placement and for major classroom disruptions.

Step 12.   Determine when and how BIAs will be used (see Chapter 4).

Major Focus: BIAs are used after the ICU has been ineffective. The classroom teacher should write the BIA. If the BIA is broken, a principal BIA can be designed.

Step 13.   Develop procedures for informing parents of the RCM plan. (See the middle school model later in this chapter.)

Major Focus: Parents need to be informed and encouraged to participate. We suggest that the middle school parent package include the following:
1. Letter from the principal (see Figure 5–4)
2. Open House or Parent Meeting to answer questions
3. Copies of the school standard, guidelines, and consequences
4. Letter from the individual teacher or teaching team listing and explaining the classroom or grade-level guidelines and procedures
5. Explanation of logical consequences, ICU, and BIA, which are provided by the DRC and/or Administrative Team
6. Form for parents and students to sign indicating that they understand the program

FIGURE 5–4

Letter from the Principal Introducing RCM to Middle School Parents

---

Dear Parents,

This school year at Jones Middle School, we will be implementing the Responsible Classroom Management (RCM) plan. RCM is an exciting and creative approach for teaching responsibility to students while effectively managing classroom behavior. RCM is based on the following assumptions:

1. The majority of students do not require disciplinary action by teacher.
2. Teachers are professionals who are responsible individuals capable of promoting responsibility in students.
3. Responsibility can be taught to any student, regardless of family or socioeconomic factors.
4. Maximum results can be achieved when teachers provide active and interactive instruction with high expectations to responsible students.
5. Students can be taught to resolve conflict and to solve adult and peer problems.
6. The basic premise of RCM is that teachers can create a school and classroom climate in which students are held responsible for their actions.

If you have any questions or comments, please contact me or your child's teacher. Thank you in advance for your help and support with this program, this school, and your child.

Sincerely,

(Principal)

Step 14. Develop procedures for informing students in the middle school. (See the middle school model in this chapter.)

Major Focus: Students should be involved in the process, but at this level teachers will have to be more directive initially. We suggest that students be provided with the following:

1. Principal's introduction of the RCM plan to students by grade level or specific teams in the gym or auditorium
2. Teachers' introduction of the school standard(s), school guidelines, and grade-level or classroom guidelines
3. Discussion of ICU and BIA

Step 15. Decide if a transitional approach would be more effective in the school during the first year of using the RCM plan. (See the school-wide transition model later in this chapter.)

Major Focus: The transitional plan can be used at the beginning of the year to ease from a more external model or at any time after the beginning of the year when the RCM plan is first implemented.

Exemplary Middle School Model

In this section, we show an exemplary middle school RCM model that, like the elementary model, can be used as written or modified to meet individual school needs. The model includes the school standard and guidelines, a schoolwide discipline plan, ICU procedures, and procedures for introducing RCM to parents, students, and teachers. A sample letter for introducing RCM to parents, ICU forms, and a BIA are also included.

School Standard

I am responsible for all of my actions at Jones Middle School.

School Guidelines

Guideline 1	Students will respond to reasonable requests of adults.
Consequence	If a student does not respond to the reasonable request of an adult, the student will be assigned to the ICU.
Guideline 2	Food and drink can be consumed only in the cafeteria.
Consequence	If a student consumes food and drink outside of the cafeteria, the food or drink will be confiscated.
Guideline 3	Students will dress appropriately for the school setting.
Consequence	If a student dresses inappropriately for the school setting, the student will be sent home to change, or will change into an acceptable article of clothing from the school clothing closet, or will wear concealing outer clothing over the inappropriate article of clothing.
Guideline 4	Students will not carry bookbags at school.
Consequence	The bookbag will be confiscated.
Guideline 5	Students will adhere to all school system behavior guidelines.
Consequence	If a student fails to follow school system behavior guidelines, action will be in accordance with school system policy.

Schoolwide Discipline Plan

1. When a student breaks the standard or guideline, a consequence is given. Consequences are based on the type of behavior:

Type A.   Legal/antisocial behaviors: The student is
                                 taken to the principal.
Type B.   Inappropriate behaviors: The student is
                                 assigned to the ICU.

2. ICU standards
   - **First offense:** The student spends time in the ICU.
   - **Second offense:** The student spends time in the ICU, and
     the parent is called.
   - **Third offense:** A parent conference is conducted with the
     principal, the counselor, and the teachers who sent the student
     to the ICU on each of the three occasions.
   - **Fourth offense:** The ICU coordinator contacts the individuals
     who placed the student in the ICU each of the four times. These
     individuals write up a BIA (see Figure 5–5) and submit it to the
     DRC for approval. Copies are forwarded to all teachers who are
     involved with the BIA, the student, parents, and the principal. The
     student is also assigned to counseling with a trained counselor.
3. BIA students do not return to the ICU for any reason. They meet
   weekly or monthly with the DRC, a faculty mentor, or a student
   mentor. The DRC can modify or void the contract at any time.
4. If the BIA is broken, the student is sent to the principal by a
   member of the DRC, the teacher, or the adult who witnessed the
   infraction of the BIA.
   a. A member of the DRC, the witness of the infraction, and the
      assistant principal determine the next action. The DRC is
      informed in writing of the results. These results are filed where
      they are available for review by all certified faculty.
   b. If the student is placed on an administrative BIA, an adminis-
      trator meets with the student on a predetermined basis. If
      improvement is noted, the principal may refer the student back
      to the DRC for reconsideration.
   c. If the administrative BIA is broken, the student is suspended
      immediately, based on state law and local board policy.
   d. When the student returns to school, the following actions are
      taken:
   - The student is placed on an exclusion contract.
   - The student is assigned to counseling with a trained counselor.
   - The counselor informs the administration of the student's
     progress.
   - The counselor may recommend outside assistance that is
     within the laws of the state.
   e. If the student's behavior does not improve in counseling, the
      DRC, counselor, central office personnel, legal advisor, and
      administrative team meet to recommend the next step. This
      may include such options as alternative classes, evening
      school, alternative school, juvenile court, or expulsion.

FIGURE 5–5
Sample BIA for Middle School Students

BEHAVIOR IMPROVEMENT AGREEMENT

This is an agreement between the student and the teacher to correct undesirable behavior. No such agreement is to be used for behaviors that are prohibited by laws of the state and by school board policy. This agreement is used by a classroom teacher when the ICU has not been effective in changing the undesirable behavior. Once a student signs this contract, that student shall not return to the ICU; the consequence shall be a conference with the principal, at which time an administrative BIA shall be drawn and go into effect, or other action taken by the principal, as appropriate.

The teacher says to the student: "All other attempts to correct this undesirable and irresponsible behavior have not been successful. This agreement is the last opportunity for you to behave in a responsible manner. If you break your agreement, or if you refuse to sign it, I will refer you to the principal for further action. In addition, I would like for you to write down the actions you will take to become responsible to eliminate the undesirable behaviors that have brought you to this point. However, if you cannot or will not write down the actions you need to take, I will help you or do it for you. Then I expect you to sign this agreement and to carry it out to the best of your ability to become responsible and conduct yourself as a responsible student in our school. This agreement has three parts: promised behaviors, consequences, and signatures. The first part is what you promise to do to become responsible and eliminate the undesirable behaviors. Now write down what it is that you need to do, or let me know if I need to help you.

Promised Behaviors

My name is _____. I agree and promise to become a responsible student. Here is what I will do to become responsible:

Consequence (Read by teacher and student)

As the student entering into this agreement, I also understand that my parents and the principal will get copies of this agreement. In addition, I fully understand what will happen if I break this agreement. I understand that my teacher will notify the principal if I break my promise, and the principal will take additional action, which may include, but is not limited to, an Administrative BIA, suspension, reassignment, or legal action in an effort to help me to become responsible for my actions. Finally, I realize that I have brought this all on myself by my irresponsible actions in the past, and I know I need to change. If I do not, the worse consequence is what I do to my own life.

_____   _____
Student signature   Parent signature

Student ID# _____   Grade _____   Date _____

Original to Teacher   Copy to Student, Parent, File, Principal, Counselor

---

Intensive Care Unit

When to Call

If a student does not accept responsibility for his or her actions in breaking a classroom guideline, the teacher contacts the office and asks for the ICU. The teacher gives the completed ICU referral form to the ICU staff (see Figure 5–6), who escorts the student from the classroom to the ICU.

Procedures in the ICU

1. When reporting to the ICU, students leave their personal belongings on the table.
2. The ICU coordinator files the ICU referral form (see Figure 5–6).
3. Students sit down and face the wall while in the ICU.

FIGURE 5–6
ICU Referral Form for Middle School Students

ICU Referral Form

Student _____   Teacher _____

Class Period _____   Date _____

Please provide the following information before the student goes to the ICU if at all possible. Circle the number of the expectation that the student did not follow, and give a brief description.

1.   Students will respond to reasonable requests of adults.

2.   Students will follow posted classroom guidelines.

Comment:

_____

_____

_____

_____

_____

_____

Please list the interventions you have attempted before this referral to the ICU.

_____

_____

_____

_____

---

4. If students do not correct their behavior while in the ICU, the principal or an assistant principal will intervene.
5. If students do not follow ICU guidelines, they may not exit.

Length of Stay in the ICU

A student should remain in the ICU for a minimum of one class period unless an administrator or ICU coordinator makes a different judgment.

ICU Monitor Responsibilities

1. Monitor students to ensure that they follow the "no talking" guideline.
2. Keep a file for every student assigned to the ICU.
3. Students should fill out an exit form (see Figure 5–7) before returning to class. File one copy in the student's discipline folder; the other copy goes to the referring teacher.

Inappropriate Reasons for Assignment to ICU

The ICU should not be overused; this renders it ineffective. Therefore, students should not be sent to the ICU for minor infractions such as (1) chewing gum or eating candy, (2) lacking materials for class, or (3) tardiness. After-school detention may be considered for these problems.

The RCM classroom is built on mutual trust between teacher and students.

FIGURE 5–7
ICU Exit Form for Middle School Students

ICU Exit Form

Student Name _____ Date _____

I am responsible for all of my actions.

My irresponsible actions were:

_____

_____

_____

_____

_____

_____

My commitment to become a responsible student is:

_____

_____

_____

_____

_____

_____

ICU monitor comments:

THE SECONDARY SCHOOL PLAN

Steps for Implementation

In implementing the secondary school schoolwide model, the following steps should be used:

Step 1. Review how the RCM plan differs from other classroom management models (see Chapter 1).

Major Focus: Using the RCM plan, educators teach students how to be responsible and allow students to self-correct inappropriate behavior.

Step 2.   Review the major aspects of growth and development, focusing primarily on the adolescent years (see Chapter 2).

Major Focus: Children go through various stages of growth and development. Review how these different stages of development impact learning and classroom behavior.

Step 3.   Review the major principles of the RCM plan, and analyze the major research findings of the pilot and model RCM schools (see Chapter 3).

Major Focus: RCM is research-based and has a high degree of success when the principles of the model are followed completely.

Step 4.   Design a warm and inviting school for all students (see Chapter 3).

Major Focus: An inviting environment is conducive to higher motivation and learning. It helps build a sense of community.

Step 5.   Establish the school standard(s) (see Chapter 4).

Major Focus: Either the full faculty or an elected DRC determines the school standard(s). Input from parents and students is strongly encouraged. We recommend that one school standard be used initially. The most effective standard has been "I am responsible for all my actions."

Step 6.   Establish school guidelines that are to be monitored by the entire faculty and staff.

Major Focus: School guidelines focus more on behavior outside of the classroom, especially in hall, lunchroom, and outside situations. However, these can focus on behaviors such as disrespect or vulgarity in the classroom. In this case, a school guideline (such as respect) is automatically part of the classroom plan. A school guideline can be used as the first classroom guideline.

Step 7.   Develop one specific consequence for each school guideline (see Chapter 4).

Major Focus: The process of developing specific consequences will keep all of the faculty and staff focused on a schoolwide model. Every adult should work in harmony—no territorial protection. For example, if a tenth-grade English teacher sees a violation of a school guideline by a senior, she enforces the consequences.

Step 8.   Each teacher or content team develops guidelines for individual classrooms (see Chapter 4).

Major Focus: Teachers work in a democratic process with students to determine specific guidelines. When the program is first implemented by a school, teachers will provide more structure and direct suggestions for the process. These guidelines are posted in the classroom underneath the school standard(s).

Step 9.   Create a collection of logical consequences for classroom or departmental use (see Chapter 4).

Major Focus: Classroom consequences are not posted; instead, the teacher has numerous consequences that can be individualized for maximum effectiveness.

Step 10.   Develop a classroom instructional plan that introduces the concept of responsibility as RCM is implemented. Responsibility, character development, and civility should be integrated in appropriate instructional situations throughout the year, especially in social studies (see Chapter 4).

Major Focus: The more responsibility is taught and expected, the greater the effectiveness of the plan.

Step 11.   Establish a schoolwide ICU complete with a schedule, personnel, and procedures (see Chapter 4).

Major Focus: The ICU is used schoolwide for behaviors that require ICU placement and for major classroom disruptions.

Step 12.   Determine when and how BIAs will be used (see Chapter 4).

Major Focus: BIAs are used after the ICU has been ineffective. The classroom teacher should write the BIA. If the BIA is broken, a DRC BIA can be designed.

Step 13.   Procedures for informing parents of the RCM plan must be developed. (See the secondary school model later in this chapter.)

Major Focus: Parents need to be informed and encouraged to participate. We suggest that the secondary school parent package include the following:
   1. Letter from the principal
   2. Open House or Parent Meeting to answer questions
   3. Copy of the school standard(s), guidelines, and consequences
   4. Letter from the individual teacher or teaching team listing and explaining the classroom or grade-level guidelines and procedures
   5. Explanations of logical consequences, ICU, and BIA, which are provided by the DRC and/or Administrative Team
   6. A form for parents and students to sign indicating that they understand the program

Step 14.   Develop procedures for informing students in the secondary school. (See the secondary school model later in this chapter.)

Major Focus: Students should be involved in the process, but teachers will have to be more directive initially. We suggest that students be provided with the following:
   1. Principal's introduction of the RCM plan to students by grade level or specific teams in the gym or auditorium

2. Teachers' or teams' introduction to students of the school standard(s), school guidelines, and departmental or individual classroom guidelines
3. Discussion of the ICU and BIA

Step 15.   Decide if a transitional approach would be more effective in the school during the first year of using the RCM plan. (See the transition model later in this chapter.)

Major Focus: The transitional plan can be used at the beginning of the year to ease from a more external model or at any time after the beginning of the year when the RCM plan is first implemented.

Exemplary Secondary School Model

This section provides an exemplary secondary school RCM model that, like the preceding models, can be used as written or modified to meet individual school needs. The model includes the school standard and guidelines, classroom guidelines, faculty and staff procedures, ICU and BIA procedures, and a description of the DRC.

School Standard

As a student at Davis High School, I am responsible for all my actions.

School Guidelines

Guideline 1	The following major offenses are considered illegal and will not be tolerated: fighting, substance abuse, vandalism, stealing, threats to any adult, bringing weapons to school, and a physical attack on any adult.
Consequence	The parent or guardian will be notified immediately. Law enforcement officials may be notified and legal charges sought against offenders. Additionally, suspension and/or expulsion will be included in the consequence.
Guideline 2	Students must exhibit responsible behavior while driving on school grounds.
Consequence	Students will be taken immediately to the principal when they return to the campus. School parking privileges will be revoked for one year.
Guideline 3	The school grounds are considered an extension of the school. Students must

	always be in appropriate areas at designated times.
Consequence	The observing adult takes the student to the ICU for the remainder of the period and/or the next period.
Guideline 4	Students will exhibit responsible cafeteria and lunch period behavior at all times.
Consequence	The observing adult takes the student to the ICU.
Guideline 5	Students must exhibit appropriate responsible behavior in the halls just as is expected in the classroom.
Consequence	The observing adult takes the student to the ICU.

Classroom Guidelines

Each teacher will establish individual guidelines. However, sample ninth- or tenth-grade classroom guidelines follow. Classroom guidelines will be posted in rooms:

To be a responsible person in this class, I will

1. Come to class prepared with necessary materials.
2. Not use profanity or vulgarity.
3. Respect my fellow students and teacher and follow the teacher's directions.

The teacher may add to the list of classroom guidelines and should send a letter home with each student on the first day stating the guidelines. No consequences are posted or defined in any letters to parents.

Faculty Procedures: Enforcing School Guidelines

The following list specifies the procedures that faculty will use when students break a school guideline. It also expands on the school guidelines that concern inappropriate behaviors.

Guidelines 1, 2	Illegal or antisocial behaviors
Consequence	The teacher takes the student to the principal's office immediately or calls the office for help.

Guidelines 3 to 5 concern inappropriate behavior. The consequence for students breaking these guidelines is assignment to the ICU.

Guideline 3	Students are not allowed outside the building between 8:15 AM and 3:00 PM

	without a pass. All students need to report immediately to the building on arrival at school. After 8:15, all students need to report to the building at the office door. All students who are checking out should leave through the office door. All students who are not involved in extracurricular activities need to clear the building and parking lot by 3:15 (making a responsible effort to leave).
Guideline 4	All students will remain in the cafeteria, gym lobby, and/or extended area outside the cafeteria. Students must have a pass to go to the office, guidance office, library, or their locker. Students must not cut in front of others in the lunch line.
Guideline 5	Students should observe proper hall behavior. Hall passes must be used by any student in the halls. Teachers should have three wooden passes to be used by students who need to leave their classrooms (gray for the hall, black for the rest room, and white for the ICU).
Behavior in the ICU	Students sit in straight-backed chairs. No talking is allowed. Students are not allowed to do anything other than sit or read provided materials. Students must leave all books and belongings at the door. Students are not allowed to leave the ICU for any reason other than a directive from the principal's office. Students will not be released before the end of a class period. The time spent in the ICU should be a minimum of 45 minutes. Less than 45 minutes will be extended to the following day for an entire class period during the same time.

Procedures for the ICU

Students will be taken to the ICU if they fail to follow the guidelines. The teacher will send for the ICU supervisor. Students will not be sent to the ICU after the third offense.

First offense: The ICU supervisor calls the student's parents.

Second offense: The ICU supervisor sets up, as soon as possible, a conference with the parents, principal, ICU supervisor, and teachers involved in both offenses. A BIA is discussed.

Third Offense: The ICU supervisor meets with the teachers involved and establishes a BIA. The ICU supervisor then submits the BIA to the DRC and sends copies to the student, parents, office, and all teachers of the student who are involved with the BIA.

Specific Duties and Information for the ICU Supervisor

The ICU supervisor or the teacher on duty should talk to the student before bringing that student to the ICU. The supervisor or teacher ensures that the student understands the reason for serving in the ICU. The supervisor or teacher explains what is expected of the student while in the ICU and answers any questions, ensuring that the student is aware of the length of time that the student will serve (all period, or if less than 45 minutes, the student returns the following day to serve all period during that same period).

If a student is completing time from another day, this is recorded as one offense, not two separate offenses, which is noted on the ICU referral form.

A review committee monitors records each week to identify patterns and possible problems.

ICU Teacher Duties

1. Fill out the ICU form in the Student Record notebook. Provide all requested information.
2. If a student will not be able to serve at least 45 minutes, fill out a Return Form and place it in the referring teacher's box.
3. If the student is returning to complete time, add the number of minutes served on the previous day's form. (Do not record this as a separate visit.)
4. Please do not leave the room unless you have someone to cover for you.
5. If you cannot serve, ask someone to cover for you. Leave duties and plans for the substitute when you are absent.
6. If directed by an administrator: For students who are late to class or school, record the date and time; sign the admission slip and send the student to class; fill out the tardy card located in the green file box behind the desk. Call students on the absence list when no students are in the ICU.
7. The phone should not be used for anything except school business.

Discipline Review Committee

The DRC will review BIAs; establish and maintain an up-to-date list of students on BIAs; and send copies to teachers. The DRC sets up a meeting with BIA students; BIA students never return to the ICU. The DRC assigns the student a faculty or student mentor to meet with the student periodically.

The DRC can modify or void the BIA at any time that it determines that the student's behavior has changed. The DRC will refer any student not following the BIA to the principal. The principal and the DRC will then determine the action to be taken. This may be an administrative BIA, suspension, or counseling. The DRC will be informed in writing of the results; these are filed where all certified faculty may review them. The DRC will meet weekly or as needed.

Administrative BIA

Teacher-prepared BIAs are established for any student who has been sent to the ICU three times. If the student breaks that BIA, the principal prepares an administrative BIA. The administrator meets with the student on a predetermined basis. If improvement is noticed, the administrator may refer the student back to the DRC for reconsideration.

If the administrative BIA is broken, the student is suspended immediately, based on state law and local board policy. When the student returns to school, the student is assigned to a daily group/individual counseling session with a trained counselor. If the student's behavior does not improve in counseling, the administrative team recommends the next step.

Specific Duties and Information for Teachers

Student Pass

Each teacher stores three wooden passes for student use: black is for the rest room, white is for the ICU, gray is for the hall.

Lunch Duties

Teachers will not allow students to bring food or drinks outside the cafeteria. Teachers on duty will rotate eating times. During lunch, students will exit the cafeteria through the doors at the gym lobby. They may enter the doors at the science wing, but they may not exit through those doors. Teachers will give passes to students who need to go to the library or office.

Tardiness

Students will go to the principal's office on first entry. They will receive a pass from the office to class. Students late for class will be considered "in the hall without a pass."

Classroom

- Teachers should handle everything they can by themselves in their classrooms.
- Teachers should try not to overuse the ICU.

- Teachers should be careful with guidelines such as "no gum" and "be prepared." They should try other things, such as contracts.
- Teachers should not watch the clock and send students to the ICU at a certain time just so they will have to serve again on the following day.
- Teachers should contact the parents when sending a student from class. If several phone calls result in no contact, the teacher should document each call.
- If the student is sent from other areas, the ICU supervisor will contact the parents.
- On a student's third ICU visit, a conference will be scheduled with parents and any teachers involved plus at least one administrator.
- Teachers must have a conference with the student after each ICU session.
- Behavior contracts can be used to help in the classroom.
- If the teacher cannot do ICU or lunch duty, it is the teacher's responsibility to see that the duty is covered. No one should be left short-handed. Teachers should try to handle some of the smaller problems in the classroom.

SCHOOLWIDE TRANSITIONS FROM OTHER STUDENT MANAGEMENT MODELS

As we have stated, the faculty may desire to ease into the program by establishing a transition from the school's old model of discipline to the RCM plan. This approach should be used only temporarily before moving fully into the complete RCM plan. The DRC should not be used in the transition model. More of the decisions are determined by individual teachers.

The procedures for establishing schoolwide standards are described in Chapter 4. The principal should lead the faculty in determining the acceptable types of guidelines for classroom use with school standards. Types of acceptable consequences for a variety of inappropriate behaviors should be clearly delineated. In addition, procedures for placement and monitoring of students in the ICU should be established. Next, procedures for using BIAs must be determined, with guidance provided by the principal in appropriate types of consequences to be used on teacher BIAs.

The principal and faculty should then present the RCM plan to parents by letter and in an open meeting format, such as in a PTA meeting. The opportunity to discuss how this program differs from other programs previously used at the school should be provided. Input from parents should be solicited with respect to their expectations for student responsibility. In addition, parents should be encouraged to use principles of the plan in their discipline of children at home.

Steps for Implementation

Within each individual classroom, the following steps should be employed by every teacher in implementing the transitional plan:

Step 1. Send a letter to parents at the time of the transition informing them of the school's new approach. Parents should sign and return the form, thereby stating that they understand the RCM plan. Encourage parents to recommend any types of desirable behaviors that they would like to be included in the plan.

Step 2. Review with the students the intention to change the discipline plan for the classroom, especially if the school year has already started. If it is the beginning of the year, inform students that the school will be using a discipline plan much different from those that they have experienced.

Step 3. Conduct class meetings in which the class discusses what it means to be a responsible student in the school and in class. Record student comments on the board.

Step 4. Explain that the school is eliminating rules and replacing these with standards and guidelines and that student ideas will be incorporated into the plan.

Step 5. State the school's predetermined standard. The most successful has been, "I am responsible for all my actions." Students share how their ideas about responsible behavior can be incorporated into the class plan.

Step 6. State three or four predetermined guidelines (specific behaviors that teachers expect from responsible students). Then the students identify two or three suggestions from the class-developed list to be included as guidelines. Student guidelines that do not match school or classroom expectations must not be accepted. An example of a teacher guideline is "Responsible students come to class prepared to learn." A possible student guideline might be "Responsible students respect the private property of other students." We suggest that in the transition approach no more than one standard and three guidelines be used.

Step 7. Send a copy of the school standard and classroom guidelines home for parents to keep for reference.

Step 8. Do not post consequences. However, develop a list of predetermined consequences that can be used when guidelines are not followed. Spontaneity of consequences will come more naturally with time and practice.

Step 9. Use directives in the same manner as stated in the complete model.

Step 10.   Use the ICU and BIAs in the same manner as stated in the
complete model.

As one can see, much of the RCM plan is used during the transition.
One difference is that the teacher has predetermined the standard and several of the related guidelines. Additionally, the teacher has predetermined
consequences for use until the teacher becomes proficient in developing
consequences that are a natural result of individual incidents. Ultimately,
the teacher wants to move students into the full model, which allows students to have greater input into the development of standards and guidelines. This may come after three weeks or three months. It will depend on
the level of responsibility students are developing and on the teacher's consistency in applying appropriate consequences.

A word of caution: The teacher should be careful that the students do
not recognize that the teacher has predetermined consequences for any particular inappropriate behavior. It is important to maintain flexibility and
professionalism to base student discipline on their individual needs.

RCM FOR TEACHING TEAMS AND
INDIVIDUAL CLASSROOMS

In the RCM school model, an ICU room is established with the support of
the school's administration and monitored by school personnel. When
sending a child to the ICU, the teacher calls an assistant or volunteer to
escort the child from the classroom to the ICU. Teams or individual classroom teachers can establish a similar arrangement with a group of interested teachers.

Intensive Care Unit

Perhaps the principal could find an area where a group of four or five teachers set up a small ICU area, possibly in an unused or seldom used office, a
storage room, or the end of a hall. As a team, teachers establish procedures
using assistants and volunteers to monitor the area. Once a child is sent to
the ICU, the monitor has the child sit quietly. One exception: The monitor
can ask the child about what has happened in order to allow the child to
ventilate frustration. The monitor says nothing else and makes no judgments verbally or nonverbally. Just as in the classroom model, the teacher
should confer with the student at the earliest convenience and complete
the ICU referral form. The teacher should give a copy of the form to the
principal in this case. Our research indicates that the ICU is more effective
if no work is assigned to students in the ICU.

Note: If an individual teacher is unable to develop an arrangement with another teacher, *no ICU is used. Teachers must not set up an ICU within the classroom.* The intention is to remove the child completely from the environment to restore order. Teachers in this situation should bypass the ICU and go straight to the BIA.

Steps for Implementation

Step 1. Review how the RCM plan differs from other classroom management models (see Chapter 1).

Major Focus: Using the RCM plan, educators teach students how to be responsible and allow students to self-correct inappropriate behavior.

Step 2. Review the major aspects of growth and development, placing the greatest focus on the appropriate age range (see Chapter 2).

Major Focus: Children go through various stages of growth and development. Review how these different stages of development impact learning and classroom behavior.

Step 3. Review the major principles of the RCM plan, and analyze the major research findings of the pilot and model RCM schools (see Chapter 3).

Major Focus: RCM is research-based and has a high degree of success when the principles of the model are followed completely. This is true in both team and individual classroom settings.

Step 4. Design a warm and inviting classroom for all students (see Chapter 3).

Major Focus: An inviting environment is conducive to higher motivation and learning. It helps build a sense of community.

Step 5. Establish the team or classroom standard(s) (see Chapter 4).

Major Focus: Determine the classroom standard, either in a team meeting or individually. Input from parents and students is strongly encouraged. We recommend that one school standard be used initially. The most effective standard has been "I am responsible for all my actions."

Step 6. Establish classroom guidelines that are to be monitored by the team or other staff members.

Major Focus: These guidelines focus specifically on the classroom. However, guidelines can be used for behavior in the hall, lunchroom, and playground situations. Teachers should work in a democratic process with students to determine specific guidelines. When the program is first used by a team or individual classroom, the teacher should provide more structure and direct suggestions for the process. These guidelines are posted in the classroom underneath the team or classroom standard(s) (see Chapter 4).

Step 7.   Create a collection of logical consequences for classroom or team level use (see Chapter 4).

Major Focus: Classroom consequences are not posted; instead, the team or teacher has numerous consequences that can be individualized for maximum effectiveness.

Step 8.   Develop a classroom instructional plan that introduces the concept of responsibility as RCM is implemented. Responsibility, character development, and civility should be integrated in appropriate instructional situations throughout the year (see Chapter 4).

Major Focus: The more responsibility is taught and expected, the greater the effectiveness of the plan.

Step 9.   Establish a team ICU complete with procedures (see Chapter 5). The ICU is not used within a classroom.

Major Focus: The ICU is used for behaviors that are major classroom disruptions.

Step 10.   Determine when and how BIAs will be used (see Chapter 4).

Major Focus: BIAs are used after the ICU has been ineffective. The classroom teacher should write the BIA. If the BIA is broken, a principal BIA can be designed.

Step 11.   Develop procedures for informing parents of the RCM plan.

Major Focus: Parents need to be informed and encouraged to participate. We suggest that the parent package include the following:
   1. Letter from the teacher
   2. Open Classroom or Parent Meeting to answer questions
   3. Copy of the classroom standard(s), guidelines, and procedures
   4. Explanation of logical consequences, ICU, and BIA
   5. A form for parents and students to sign indicating that they understand the program

Note: If a team or individual teacher desires to start the program during the year, the basic procedures from the schoolwide transition model can be used. We suggest that for a classroom situation RCM should begin at only two times: the beginning of the year or after the holidays.

PUTTING CONCEPTS INTO PRACTICE

Class Activity

The class assumes the role of a group of faculty members. Develop a school model, and go through the procedures of establishing the RCM plan. Establish school and classroom standards. To start, the instructor divides the class into nongraded level groups.

Direct each group to determine the behavior standards for the school. Once each group has two or three standards, divide the groups into grade levels, and ask them to finalize one standard for the school. After each group has determined one standard, a member from each group writes it on the board. Discuss each standard and, by the process of eliminating or combining, decide on one or two standards for the school. Next, move to school guidelines, school consequences, grade-level guidelines, and a pool of the consequences.

Establish an ICU, complete with a schedule, personnel, and procedures. Determine how and when BIAs will be used.

Intensive Care Register

Intensive Care Register

Date_____   Supervisor's Time

ICU Supervisors _____   In _____   Out _____

                 _____   In _____   Out _____

                 _____   In _____   Out _____

                 _____   In _____   Out _____

                 _____   In _____   Out _____

	Student	Teacher	Time In	Time Out	Comments
1					
2					
3					
4					
5					
6					
7					
8					
9					
10					

Reviewed by Assistant Principal or Principal

Signature _____ Date _____

APPENDIX **B**

Individual Student
ICU Report

Individual Student ICU Report

Date _____   ICU Supervisor _____

Time in ICU: _____ to _____   Visit #1_____ 2_____ 3_____

Student's Name   _____

Homeroom Teacher   _____

Grade Level   _____

Recommending Teacher   _____

_____

Specific Problem Requiring ICU Placement

_____

Student's Response

_____

Required Behavior Upon Returning to Class

_____

Teacher's Signature   _____

Student's Signature   _____

                Copy to:

                Parents (mailed)   _____

                Principal   _____

                Homeroom Teacher   _____

                Recommending Teacher   _____

Behavior Improvement Agreements

BEHAVIOR IMPROVEMENT AGREEMENT
TEACHER

Student _____   Homeroom Teacher _____

ID # _____   Recommending Teacher _____

Grade/Class _____   Date _____

PROMISED BEHAVIORS

I, _____, **agree** and **promise** to do the following:

Failure to keep this agreement will result in the issuance of the following consequences:

CONSEQUENCES

SIGNATURES

_____   _____
Student   Teacher

BEHAVIOR IMPROVEMENT AGREEMENT
PRINCIPAL

Student _____

Homeroom Teacher _____

ID # _____

Recommending Teacher _____

Grade/Class _____

Date _____

PROMISED BEHAVIORS

I, _____, **agree** and **promise** to do the following:

Failure to keep this agreement will result in the issuance of the following consequences:

CONSEQUENCES

SIGNATURES

_____

Student

_____

Principal/Designee

RCM Discipline Plan— ICU Referral Form

RCM Discipline Referral Form—ICU Referral Form

Student _____ Date_____

Period _____ Subject _____ Referring Teacher _____

Outside Areas

_____ 1. Outside at unauthorized times
_____ 2. Unsupervised areas
_____ 3. Littering

Halls

_____ 1. Overt sexual behavior
_____ 2. Foul language
_____ 3. Running in hall/horseplay
_____ 4. No pass
_____ 5. Disruptive behavior during lunch

Cafeteria

_____ 1. In unauthorized areas during lunch
_____ 2. Cutting in line

Classroom

_____ 1. Coming to class unprepared
_____ 2. Cursing or vulgar language
_____ 3. Disrespect for teacher and/or fellow students
_____ 4. Not following directions
_____ 5. Failure to follow teacher's RCM Plan

Comments:

Signature of Student _____

Signature of ICU Supervisor _____

Distribution: Referring Teacher
ICU

Index